BLOCKCHAIN FOR TOURISM AND HOSPITALITY INDUSTRIES

This insightful book is the first to explain the basics of blockchain and its applications in the service industry, as well as potential future implementations of the technology.

Embellished with explanatory diagrams throughout, this book predominantly focuses on blockchain as a prominent driver of digital transformation within the service sector and explores its potential applications within the tourism and hospitality industries. Expert-led and logically structured, the chapters explore a plethora of concepts within the service industry and explain the possibilities of blockchain technology and its pros and cons. Key topics include blockchain and its current and potential future impact on food and agricultural supply chains, the sharing economy, non-fungible tokens (NFTs), financial systems and payments, medical tourism, sustainability, and smart contracts. The book seeks to inspire and influence industry figures to plan ahead and develop business strategies using blockchain.

International in scope, this engaging volume will be of pivotal interest to industry experts as well as researchers and tourism, hospitality, and technology students interested in learning more about blockchain and its potential for the service industry.

Irem Onder is an associate professor at the Department of Hospitality and Tourism Management at University of Massachusetts Amherst. She obtained her PhD from Clemson University, South Carolina, and her master's degree in information systems management from Ferris State University, Michigan. Her main research interests include information technology and tourism economics, specifically big data analysis, smart destinations, decision support systems, blockchain, and tourism demand forecasting. She serves in the editorial boards of *Journal of Travel Research*, *Tourism Economics*, and *Journal of Information Technology and*

Tourism. Her research has been published in journals such as *Annals of Tourism Research, Tourism Management, Journal of Travel Research, Tourism Economics*, and *Journal of Information Technology and Tourism*.

Fulya Acikgoz is a PhD candidate at the University of Bristol, UK. Her research focuses on technology marketing, information management, and social media. Her work has been published in journals, including *Journal of Business Research, Psychology & Marketing, Technovation, International Journal of Contemporary Hospitality Management, International Journal of Consumer Studies, Journal of Business & Industrial Marketing, Behaviour & Information Technology, International Journal of Human–Computer Interaction, Journal of Marketing for Higher Education*, and *International Journal of Technology Marketing*.

BLOCKCHAIN FOR TOURISM AND HOSPITALITY INDUSTRIES

Edited by
Irem Onder and Fulya Acikgoz

Routledge
Taylor & Francis Group

LONDON AND NEW YORK

Designed cover image: iStock / bymuratdeniz

First published 2024
by Routledge
4 Park Square, Milton Park, Abingdon, Oxon OX14 4RN

and by Routledge
605 Third Avenue, New York, NY 10158

Routledge is an imprint of the Taylor & Francis Group, an informa business

British Library Cataloguing-in-Publication Data
A catalogue record for this book is available from the British Library

ISBN: 978-1-032-39903-4 (hbk)
ISBN: 978-1-032-39904-1 (pbk)
ISBN: 978-1-003-35191-7 (ebk)

DOI: 10.4324/9781003351917

Typeset in Times New Roman
by codeMantra

CONTENTS

FIGURES

TABLES

CONTRIBUTORS

Dr. Dorin-Cristian Coita is an associate professor at the University of Oradea, Romania, teaching and researching in the field of Marketing, Services Marketing, Tourism Marketing, Management and Marketing of Nonprofit Organizations. His research interests are social innovation, blockchain, organization development.

Dr. Engin Demirel is a professor of finance in the Faculty of Economics and Administrative Sciences at Trakya University. He received his master degree (MA) in the field of Finance (Options Pricing) in 2005 from Trakya University and Doctorate (Ph.D.) (Fixed Income Securities Portfolio Optimization) in Accounting and Finance in 2009 from Marmara University. He teaches finance courses at graduate and undergraduate levels. His research interests include financial markets and institutions, portfolio optimizations and international finance. Demirel has published four books, book chapters, and articles in national and international journals.

Fulya Acikgoz is a PhD candidate at the University of Bristol, UK. Her research focuses on technology marketing, information management, and social media.

Dr. Olimpia Iuliana Ban is a full professor and PhD coordinator in the field of Business Administration at the Faculty of Economic Sciences, University of Oradea. She is also a national project manager in Romania. Her research interests focus on tourist destinations, customer satisfaction of tourism services, and smart tourism.

Tolga Benli is a research assistant and PhD student at the Department of Business, Atilim University, Turkey. His research interests are sustainability in supply chains, blockchain-based supply chains, renewable energy, and financial management.

Dr. Ismail Erol is a full-professor at Baskent University in Turkey and has a PhD degree in Operations Management. He has published research in various academic journals. His research interests are circularity and sustainability in supply chains, disruptive technologies, and quantitative decision analyses.

Dr. Ulrike Gretzel is a lecturer at the Institute for Tourism, Wine Business, and Marketing in the IMC University of Applied Sciences Krems, Austria. Her research focuses on the design, use, and implications of emerging technologies.

Muhiba Ahmed Khan is a PhD student at Atilim University in the Department of Business. Her research interests are as follows: supply chain optimization, circular supply chain management, sustainable supply chain management, and artificial intelligence in supply chain excellence.

Erdita Kumaraku is a student at Epoka University, Albania, where she is currently in her third year of the Business Informatics program. In addition to her studies, her specific research interests include network security protocols and risk assessment methodologies.

Dr. İ. Tolga Medeni is a full professor at Ankara Yildirim Beyazit University in Turkey and has a PhD degree in Computer Engineering. His research interests are digital transformation in supply chains, blockchain-based supply chains, and optimization.

Dr. Tunç Medeni is a full professor at Ankara Yildirim Beyazit University in Turkey and has a PhD degree in knowledge management. His research interests are knowledge and technology management in supply chains, e-government, and operational excellence.

Dr. Irem Onder is an associate professor at the University of Massachusetts Amherst. Her research focuses on technology and its impact on the tourism industry, specifically blockchain and big data.

Dr. Marc Pilkington is currently Associate Professor of Economics at the University of Burgundy Franche Comté, France. In 2021–2022, he was on secondment as Associate Professor of Business Administration at Epoka University, Albania, where he served as Dean of the Faculty of Economics and Administrative Science (FEAS). His current interests lie in blockchain technology, heterodox monetary macroeconomics, tourism, higher education systems, and post-Soviet economies.

Dr. Nikolaos Stylos is a senior lecturer in Marketing (Grade L, Assoc. Prof.) and member of the Marketing & Consumption Academic Group at the University of Bristol Business School, UK. His research interests are smart tourism, hospitality, and the economy; online platforms; and big data to support various collaborative consumption models pertaining to tourists' accommodation, transportation, and activities and their respective implications for sustainability.

Dr. Horst Treiblmaier is Full Professor and Head of the Department of International Management. His research interests include implications of blockchain and distributed ledger technology, gamification, as well as epistemological and methodological issues.

Dr. Seda Karagoz Zeren is a research assistant at Department of Business Administration, Faculty of Economics and Administrative Sciences, Trakya University. Her research focuses on tourism technologies, sustainability, tourism management, tourism finance, and interdisciplinary approaches.

PREFACE

Dear Reader,

It is with great pleasure and excitement that we present to you this edited volume, *Blockchain for Tourism and Hospitality Industries*. As the editors, we have had the privilege of working with a talented group of contributors to bring together a diverse collection of insights and perspectives on blockchain technology and its impacts on tourism and hospitality industries. This book represents a collaborative effort aimed at illuminating various aspects of blockchain from multiple angles.

The idea for this edited volume emerged from a desire to foster a rich dialogue among experts, scholars, and practitioners in the field of blockchain. It is a testament to the collective knowledge and expertise within our community, and we are humbled by the wealth of ideas and experiences that these individuals have shared.

Within the pages of *Blockchain for Tourism and Hospitality Industries* you will find a collection of thought-provoking chapters, each authored by a respected specialist in their respective field. These contributions offer unique insights, in-depth analyses, and practical applications that contribute to a comprehensive understanding of blockchain technology. Through the diversity of perspectives presented, we hope to inspire new ideas, challenge existing paradigms, and encourage further exploration.

Chapter 1 provides a comprehensive introduction to blockchain technology, explaining its core concepts, underlying principles, and benefits and challenges.

Chapter 2 examines the intersection of blockchain and the hospitality and tourism industry. This chapter explores how blockchain can enhance transparency, streamline booking processes, and improve customer experiences, ultimately transforming the way the industry operates.

With a focus on the food supply chain, Chapter 3 discusses the potential of blockchain technology to improve traceability, reduce fraud, and enhance food safety in the hospitality and tourism sector, providing consumers with greater confidence in the origin and quality of the products they consume.

Exploring the impact of blockchain on the sharing economy, Chapter 4 investigates how distributed ledger technology can facilitate peer-to-peer transactions, enhance trust, and enable secure and transparent sharing of resources within the tourism and hospitality space.

Chapter 5 delves into the emerging concept of non-fungible tokens (NFTs) and their implications for the tourism industry. It explores how NFTs can be used to tokenize unique experiences, artworks, and digital assets, creating new opportunities for tourism businesses and travelers alike.

Highlighting the role of blockchain in revolutionizing payment systems, Chapter 6 examines the potential of cryptocurrencies and blockchain-based payment platforms to provide faster, more secure, and cost-effective transactions within the tourism and hospitality sector.

Exploring the intersection of blockchain and medical tourism, Chapter 7 investigates medical tourism in Albania and examines the industry, specifically how distributed ledgers can enhance patient data security, streamline medical records management, and improve trust and transparency in cross-border healthcare services.

Chapter 8 explores the concept of tokenization of physical assets and its application in the tourism industry. It discusses how blockchain technology enables the fractional ownership of assets, such as tourist attractions, allowing for increased liquidity and investment opportunities within the tourism sector, which can also help sustainability of these tourism attractions.

Focusing on smart contracts, Chapter 9 provides an in-depth analysis of their capabilities and potential use cases in the tourism and hospitality industry. It explores how self-executing contracts can automate processes, enforce agreements, and enhance efficiency and trust in various tourism-related transactions, which also contribute to sustainable tourism.

In the final chapter, the book explores the future prospects and potential disruptions that blockchain technology may bring to the tourism and hospitality industry. It discusses emerging trends, challenges, and opportunities, highlighting the transformative impact that blockchain is expected to have on shaping the industry's landscape in the years to come.

We extend our deepest gratitude to each contributor for their exceptional dedication and commitment to this project. Their expertise and passion have shaped the contents of this book, making it a valuable resource for researchers, students, and professionals alike. Their willingness to share their knowledge and engage in scholarly discourse is commendable, and we are immensely grateful for their contributions.

It is important to note that this book represents a snapshot of the current state of knowledge in the field of blockchain technology. Given the ever-evolving nature of research and scholarship, new discoveries and perspectives will undoubtedly emerge. We hope that this volume will serve as a foundation for further exploration and stimulate future investigations in the field.

As you embark on this intellectual journey, we encourage you to approach each chapter with an open mind, ready to engage with diverse perspectives and challenge your own assumptions. It is my sincere hope that the ideas presented within these pages will inspire and enrich your understanding of blockchain and how it can help tourism and hospitality, fostering new insights and encouraging further dialogue.

Thank you for joining us on this exciting voyage of discovery. May *Blockchain for Tourism and Hospitality Industries* serve as a catalyst for continued exploration, innovation, and advancement in the field of blockchain technology.

Warm regards,

Irem Onder and Fulya Acikgoz

1

INTRODUCTION

The Role of Technology in Transforming the Industry

Irem Onder

Technology has played a pivotal role in revolutionizing the tourism and hospitality industry, transforming the way businesses operate and how travelers plan, book, and experience their journeys. The impact of technology can be observed in various aspects of the industry, leading to enhanced efficiency, improved customer experiences, and new business opportunities. The internet, social media, and mobile devices have made it easier than ever for travelers to access information about destinations, accommodations, and attractions. Online reviews, travel blogs, and social media influencers have become crucial sources of information, empowering travelers to make informed decisions.

The emergence of online travel agencies (OTAs) and other booking platforms has simplified the booking process, offering travelers the convenience of comparing prices, availability, and options with just a few clicks. These platforms have also increased competition among businesses, driving them to improve their offerings and services. Technology has enabled businesses to collect and analyze customer data to offer personalized services and recommendations. Machine learning and artificial intelligence (AI) can help tailor marketing campaigns, suggest relevant travel packages, and improve overall customer satisfaction. It can also automate processes such as booking, check-in, and payment. AI chatbots can communicate with customers 24/7 in different languages and answer their queries. Additionally, translation apps have made it easier for travelers to communicate with locals, breaking language barriers.

Internet of Things (IoT) devices and smart technology have enhanced the guest experience in hotels and resorts. For instance, smart rooms with voice-controlled lighting, climate control, and entertainment systems offer a more comfortable and personalized stay. Smartphone apps have become indispensable travel companions, offering services such as mobile check-ins, digital boarding passes,

DOI: 10.4324/9781003351917-1

and location-based recommendations. They also enable businesses to engage with customers through push notifications and personalized offers. Virtual and augmented reality (VR/AR) technologies have enriched the travel experience by offering virtual tours, interactive maps, and immersive experiences, enabling travelers to explore destinations before they visit and enhancing their on-site experiences. VR can also provide entertainment and education for customers during their stay.

The tourism and hospitality industry has undergone a significant transformation with the help of technology. This innovative tool has been instrumental in driving improvements across various aspects of the sector, leading to remarkable advancements. However, with the continuous evolution of technology, it's imperative for the industry to adapt and harness its potential to enhance customer experiences, streamline operations, and foster sustainable growth. Therefore, technology plays a critical role in the industry's future success, and embracing its advancements is vital for staying competitive and meeting the ever-changing needs of consumers. Blockchain is one of the most promising technologies that can change the industry. According to Swan (2015), blockchain is predicted to be the fifth revolutionary computing paradigm following mainframes, PCs, the internet, and mobile/social networking.

Understanding Blockchain Technology

Blockchain technology has emerged as a groundbreaking innovation with the potential to disrupt various industries, including the tourism and hospitality sector. Initially developed as the underlying technology for Bitcoin, a digital currency, blockchain has since evolved into a versatile platform with a myriad of applications beyond cryptocurrencies. At its core, blockchain is a decentralized and distributed digital ledger that securely records transactions and data across a network of computers, known as nodes. This distributed nature of blockchain ensures transparency, security, and immutability, making it an attractive solution for numerous use cases (Crosby et al., 2016).

Key components of a blockchain include:

a *Blocks*: A block is a collection of transactions grouped together and added to the blockchain. It contains a unique identifier (hash) and a reference to the previous block, forming a chain of interconnected blocks.
b *Decentralized network*: The blockchain network consists of multiple nodes, each maintaining a copy of the entire blockchain. These nodes collaborate to validate and verify transactions, ensuring consensus without relying on a central authority.
c *Consensus mechanisms*: To achieve agreement on the validity of transactions, blockchain networks employ various consensus mechanisms, such as Proof of Work (PoW) or Proof of Stake (PoS). These mechanisms prevent fraudulent activities and ensure the integrity of the blockchain (Swan, 2015).

Blockchain technology has gained significant attention due to its potential to revolutionize various industries by streamlining processes, enhancing security, and reducing costs. In the context of tourism and hospitality, blockchain can offer innovative solutions for secure transactions, loyalty programs, supply chain management, and identity verification, among other applications. By understanding and embracing the potential of blockchain technology, businesses in the tourism and hospitality industry can stay ahead of the curve and capitalize on the opportunities presented by this transformative innovation.

How Blockchain Technology Works

Blockchain technology, with its potential to revolutionize various industries, has garnered significant attention from academia and businesses alike. To fully comprehend its implications, it is crucial to understand the underlying mechanisms that govern its functioning. In this section, we will examine the processes that enable blockchain technology to provide a secure, transparent, and decentralized ledger for recording transactions and data. The fundamental functioning of a blockchain can be understood as a series of steps involving the creation, validation, and storage of blocks that contain transactional data (Morkunas et al., 2019). The following steps provide a general outline of how a typical blockchain operates:

Initiating a transaction: A user initiates a transaction by submitting the details, such as the sender's and receiver's addresses and the transaction amount. The transaction is then broadcasted to the entire network of nodes for validation.

Verification of transactions: The nodes in the network verify the transaction details, ensuring its authenticity and checking for any discrepancies, such as double spending. This verification process may involve cross-referencing the transaction against the blockchain's historical data.

Formation of a block: Once verified, the transaction is grouped with other verified transactions to form a new block. This block also contains a reference to the previous block in the chain, establishing a chronological order of transactions.

Mining and PoW: In a PoW consensus mechanism, miners compete to solve complex mathematical problems to validate the new block. The first miner to solve the problem broadcasts the solution to the network, and other nodes verify the correctness of the solution.

Consensus and block addition: Upon verification of the solution, the nodes in the network reach consensus to accept the new block. The block is then added to the existing blockchain, and the miner who solved the problem is rewarded with a predetermined amount of cryptocurrency.

Immutable record: Once a block is added to the blockchain, its contents are considered immutable. The cryptographic linkage between blocks makes it extremely difficult to alter the data without affecting subsequent blocks, ensuring the security and integrity of the recorded transactions data (Morkunas et al., 2019).

It is important to note that the functioning of a blockchain may vary depending on the specific implementation and consensus mechanism employed. While the PoW mechanism is widely used in popular blockchains like Bitcoin and Ethereum, alternative consensus methods such as PoS and Delegated DPoS have been developed to address concerns related to energy consumption and scalability (Saad & Radzi, 2020).

Benefits and Challenges of Adopting Blockchain Technology

Blockchain technology, with its potential to transform various industries, has attracted significant interest from both academia and the business world. In the context of the tourism and hospitality industry, the adoption of blockchain technology presents a range of benefits and challenges. This section provides an exploration of the advantages and potential hurdles associated with implementing blockchain solutions in the tourism and hospitality sector.

Benefits of Blockchain Technology

Enhanced security and transparency: The decentralized and cryptographic nature of blockchain technology ensures secure and transparent transactions, fostering trust among businesses and customers. By eliminating the need for intermediaries, blockchain minimizes the risk of fraud and data manipulation, making it an attractive solution for various applications in the tourism and hospitality industry.

Cost reduction and efficiency: Blockchain's ability to automate transactions through the use of smart contracts can lead to significant cost savings and increased efficiency. By streamlining processes and reducing the need for intermediaries, businesses can optimize their operations and enhance overall customer satisfaction (Dogru et al., 2018).

Improved traceability and accountability: Blockchain's transparent and immutable ledger enables improved traceability and accountability throughout the supply chain, which is particularly relevant for the tourism and hospitality industry. Businesses can ensure the authenticity and ethical sourcing of products and services, catering to the growing demand for responsible and sustainable travel experiences.

Enhanced customer loyalty and engagement: Blockchain-based loyalty programs can offer a more seamless and secure way to manage rewards and customer engagement, providing travelers with a unified platform for earning and redeeming rewards across multiple businesses.

Identity and access management: The secure and efficient identity verification solutions offered by blockchain technology can simplify check-in processes at hotels and airports while ensuring privacy and data protection for travelers (Davidson, De Filippi, & Potts, 2016; Dogru et al., 2018).

Challenges of Adopting Blockchain Technology

Some of the challenges related to the adoption of blockchain include the following:

It's a complex technology and the implementation of blockchain technology may require significant technical expertise and resources. For many businesses in the tourism and hospitality industry, understanding and integrating this technology can be a complex and challenging process.

One of the primary concerns with blockchain technology is its scalability. As the number of transactions and participants increases, the size of the blockchain grows, which can lead to slower transaction processing times and higher resource requirements. This issue is particularly pertinent for public blockchains, such as Bitcoin and Ethereum, which have experienced network congestion and increased transaction fees during periods of high demand. Overcoming these challenges may require the development of new consensus mechanisms or the adoption of alternative blockchain platforms.

There are regulatory uncertainties. The rapidly evolving nature of blockchain technology has left regulators and policymakers grappling with the task of developing appropriate legal frameworks and guidelines. This regulatory uncertainty poses challenges for businesses and individuals looking to adopt or invest in blockchain technology, as they may face legal and compliance risks.

Industry-wide collaboration is needed to fully harness the potential of blockchain technology in the tourism and hospitality sector. This may involve overcoming barriers related to competition, standardization, and interoperability. Furthermore, for blockchain technology to deliver its full benefits, widespread adoption and network effects are necessary. However, the complex nature of the technology, coupled with a lack of understanding and misconceptions, has slowed its adoption across various industries.

Although blockchain networks offer increased transparency and security, privacy concerns still exist. Public blockchains, for instance, can expose transaction details and user information to all network participants. While this transparency is beneficial in some cases, it may not be suitable for applications that require more privacy. Various privacy-enhancing technologies, such as zero-knowledge proofs and confidential transactions, are being developed to address these concerns.

As the number of blockchain platforms and networks increases, interoperability between different blockchains becomes a significant concern. Seamless communication and data exchange between various blockchain networks are essential for realizing the technology's full potential. Efforts are being made to develop cross-chain solutions and protocols that facilitate interoperability.

There are security vulnerabilities. Despite the inherently secure nature of blockchain technology, it is not immune to security vulnerabilities. Issues such as smart contract vulnerabilities, 51% attacks, and potential quantum computing threats have raised concerns about the technology's long-term security.

In addition, the energy consumption associated with certain blockchain networks, especially those that use proof-of-work (PoW) consensus mechanisms, has raised concerns about the technology's environmental impact. PoW-based blockchains, like Bitcoin, require vast amounts of computational power and energy to validate transactions and maintain network security, contributing to increased carbon emissions. To address these concerns, PoS and Delegated PoS consensus mechanisms are developed.

Conclusion

In conclusion, blockchain technology presents a transformative paradigm that offers both challenges and tremendous benefits. While the challenges of scalability, regulatory frameworks, and energy consumption persist, the potential for enhanced security, transparency, and decentralized governance cannot be overstated. By enabling trust and verifiability in a distributed manner, blockchain has the power to revolutionize industries, streamline processes, and empower individuals. As we continue to navigate the complexities and refine the applications of blockchain, it is crucial to strike a balance between innovation and responsible implementation, fostering collaboration and interdisciplinary efforts to fully unlock the vast potential of this groundbreaking technology.

References

Crosby, M., Pattanayak, P., Verma, S., & Kalyanaraman, V. (2016). Blockchain technology: Beyond bitcoin. *Applied Innovation*, 2, 6–10.

Davidson, S., De Filippi, P., & Potts, J. (2016). *Economics of blockchain*. Available at SSRN 2744751.

Dogru, T., Mody, M., & Leonardi, C. (2018). Blockchain technology & its implications for the hospitality industry. Boston Hospitality Review, Boston University School of Hospitality Administration.

Morkunas, V. J., Paschen, J., & Boon, E. (2019). How blockchain technologies impact your business model. *Business Horizons*, 62(3), 295–306.

Saad, S. M. S., & Radzi, R. Z. R. M. (2020). Comparative review of the blockchain consensus algorithm between proof of stake (pos) and delegated proof of stake (dpos). *International Journal of Innovative Computing*, 10(2), 27–32.

Swan, M. (2015). *Blockchain: Blueprint for a new economy*. O'Reilly Media, Inc.

2

BLOCKCHAIN TECHNOLOGY IN TOURISM AND HOSPITALITY INDUSTRY

Fulya Acikgoz and Nikolaos Stylos

Introduction

The tourism and hospitality industry is a dynamic and diverse sector that holds immense significance in the global economy. It encompasses a wide array of businesses and services that cater to the needs of travelers and tourists, including accommodations, transportation, dining, attractions, entertainment, and travel agencies. This industry serves as a major catalyst for employment and revenue generation, making a substantial contribution to the gross domestic product (GDP) of numerous countries (Pedak, 2018). Over time, the tourism and hospitality industry has experienced remarkable growth, propelled by crucial factors such as globalization, increasing disposable income, and technological advancements that have enhanced the accessibility and convenience of travel. Additionally, the sector has evolved to cater to the diverse preferences of travelers, offering a multitude of experiences and services that cater to individuals on a budget as well as those seeking luxurious options.

During this process, in pursuit of their objectives, the tourism and hospitality sector has wholeheartedly embraced innovative technologies as part of their strategy. With a keen understanding of the potential benefits, the industry has actively embraced emerging solutions, including blockchain, to streamline operations and transform service delivery. In the rapidly evolving landscape of the tourism and hospitality industry, technology plays a crucial role in driving innovation and growth. It is essential for professionals in the tourism and hospitality sector to have a comprehensive understanding of blockchain technology, including its applications and implications, in order to remain competitive and thrive in the industry. The sector aims to maintain a leading position in the ever-evolving technological landscape, continuously seeking novel ways to enhance the customer experience,

DOI: 10.4324/9781003351917-2

optimize operational efficiency, and meet the changing preferences of travelers by embracing such advancement. Through the integration of groundbreaking technologies like blockchain, the tourism and hospitality sector is paving the way for a future that offers travelers a more seamless, secure, and immersive experience worldwide.

Blockchain technology has emerged as a disruptive force across various industries, and the tourism and hospitality sector is no exception. With its decentralized and secure nature, blockchain offers a range of applications and benefits that can revolutionize how businesses operate and interact within the industry. From enhancing trust and transparency in transactions to streamlining operations and improving customer experiences, the integration of blockchain technology can reshape the tourism and hospitality sector landscape. Blockchain technology, a decentralized and secure digital ledger system, has garnered increasing attention and interest across various industries. The tourism and hospitality sector is now exploring the potential applications and benefits of integrating blockchain into its operations. With its ability to enhance transparency, security, and efficiency, blockchain has the potential to revolutionize how businesses in the tourism and hospitality industry operate, interact, and deliver value to travelers.

The tourism and hospitality industry, known for its complex network of stakeholders and transactions, can significantly benefit from adopting blockchain technology. By providing a decentralized and immutable ledger, blockchain can ensure transparency and trust in various processes, including booking and payment transactions. This increased transparency can help alleviate fraud-related concerns, double bookings, and data manipulation, thereby building confidence among travelers and service providers. Furthermore, blockchain can facilitate the secure and seamless sharing of data and digital identities, enabling personalized and frictionless experiences for travelers while maintaining their privacy and control over their personal information. Additionally, the automation capabilities of blockchain, mainly with smart contracts, can streamline and simplify contractual agreements, reducing the need for intermediaries and enhancing operational efficiency in areas such as reservations, cancellations, and refunds. Overall, the integration of blockchain technology has the potential to reshape the tourism and hospitality industry by improving trust, security, efficiency, and the overall traveler experience.

According to Iansiti and Lakhani (2017), blockchain should be seen as a foundational technology rather than a disruptive one, capable of creating entirely new economic and social systems. Its gradual adoption over time necessitates the industry's understanding of its potential impact. It is crucial for the industry to explore how blockchain can be utilized to benefit both consumers and suppliers, leading to the development of innovative tourism products and systems instead of solely focusing on the technology itself.

The decentralized and transparent nature of blockchain presents unique advantages for addressing challenges faced by the tourism and hospitality sector. By incorporating blockchain solutions, professionals can streamline operations, enhance security and trust, reduce costs, and ultimately improve customer satisfaction. Key potential benefits of blockchain technology in the industry include secure and transparent transactions, blockchain-based loyalty and reward programs, efficient supply chain management and traceability, and enhanced identity and access management.

Secure and transparent transactions: Blockchain can facilitate secure, transparent, and tamper-proof transactions, which are crucial for building trust among customers and businesses. The use of smart contracts can further automate transactions, reducing the need for intermediaries and lowering transaction costs.

Loyalty and reward programs: Blockchain-based loyalty programs can offer a more seamless and secure way to manage rewards and customer engagement. These programs can be easily integrated across multiple businesses, providing travelers with a unified and easily accessible platform for earning and redeeming rewards.

Supply chain management and traceability: The transparent nature of blockchain can be leveraged for effective supply chain management, ensuring traceability and accountability throughout the entire value chain. This can help businesses improve their sustainability practices and provide customers with authentic, ethically sourced products and services.

Identity and access management: Blockchain can offer secure and efficient identity verification solutions, simplifying check-in processes at hotels and airports while ensuring privacy and data protection for travelers.

To capitalize on these opportunities, tourism and hospitality professionals must develop a thorough understanding of blockchain technology and its potential applications. This includes gaining knowledge about the technical aspects of blockchain, such as consensus mechanisms, distributed ledgers, and smart contracts, as well as the practical implications of integrating blockchain into existing operations.

Furthermore, professionals should also be aware of the potential challenges and limitations of adopting blockchain technology, such as regulatory uncertainties, technological complexities, and the need for industry-wide collaboration. By addressing these challenges and embracing the potential of blockchain technology, tourism and hospitality professionals can contribute to the development of innovative solutions that enhance the industry's efficiency, sustainability, and overall customer experience.

Blockchain Applications in the Tourism and Hospitality Industry

One illustration is the emergence of novel travel and hospitality platforms based on blockchain that use bitcoin or other cryptocurrencies as a payment method. For instance, Windingtree is a decentralized distribution platform that permits consumers to access offers directly from suppliers (Windingtree, 2020). Another application is blockchain-based loyalty programs, which can be applied to the hospitality, airline, and other tourism sectors. Such loyalty programs provide loyalty tokens as rewards to guests that can be sold or exchanged with others, and loyalty tokens of different companies can have different values, increasing competition and service quality (Dogru et al., 2018). Loyyal (loyal.com) is one such firm established for this purpose, which also aims to address the issue of accumulating sufficient points for customers to use in any organization that is part of the blockchain (Onder and Treiblmaier, 2018).

- *Secure transactions and payment processing*: Blockchain's decentralized and transparent nature makes it an ideal platform for secure and efficient payment processing. By adopting blockchain-based payment solutions, businesses can offer their customers a seamless, secure, and cost-effective means of conducting transactions, including cross-border payments and currency conversions.
- *Identity and access management*: Verifying the identity of customers is crucial in the tourism and hospitality industry, particularly for hotel check-ins and boarding at airports. Blockchain can facilitate secure, efficient, and tamper-proof identity verification solutions, simplifying these processes and enhancing customer privacy and data protection.
- *Supply chain management and traceability*: The transparent and immutable nature of blockchain makes it an ideal solution for managing supply chains in the tourism and hospitality industry. By tracking products and services from their origin to the end consumer, businesses can ensure the authenticity and ethical sourcing of their offerings. This increased traceability and accountability can help businesses cater to the growing demand for sustainable and responsible tourism experiences.
- *Smart contracts for bookings and reservations*: Blockchain-based smart contracts can automate various aspects of the booking and reservation process, reducing reliance on intermediaries and lowering transaction costs. Smart contracts can automatically execute predefined terms and conditions when specific criteria are met, streamlining the booking process and improving overall customer satisfaction.
- *Peer-to-peer travel services*: Blockchain technology can facilitate the development of decentralized, peer-to-peer platforms for various travel services, such as accommodation, transportation, and tour bookings. These platforms can enable direct interactions between service providers and customers, fostering trust and reducing transaction costs by eliminating intermediaries.
- *Reputation and review systems*: Blockchain can support the creation of transparent and tamper-proof reputation and review systems for the tourism and hospitality industry. By securely storing customer reviews on a decentralized ledger, businesses can enhance the credibility of their offerings and build trust among potential customers.
- *Decentralized booking platforms*: Decentralized booking platforms, facilitated by blockchain technology, have the potential to revolutionize the way customers access and engage with travel and hospitality services. By eliminating intermediaries such as online travel agencies (OTAs) and other third-party

platforms, decentralized booking systems can foster direct interactions between service providers and customers. This not only reduces transaction costs but also increases trust and transparency in the booking process. Furthermore, these platforms can leverage blockchain's secure and tamper-proof nature to store and manage customer reviews, reservations, and payment details, offering a seamless, efficient, and secure booking experience. As the tourism and hospitality industry continues to embrace cutting-edge technologies, decentralized booking platforms hold the promise of reshaping the industry landscape and empowering businesses and customers alike with greater control and flexibility in their travel experiences.

Potential Future Developments of Blockchain Technology in Tourism and Hospitality Industry

As blockchain technology continues to mature and evolve, its applications in the tourism and hospitality sector are expected to expand and diversify. This section presents an academic perspective on potential future developments in the intersection of blockchain and tourism, providing insights into the emerging trends and innovations that could shape the industry in the years to come.

- *Integration with the Internet of Things (IoT)*: The convergence of blockchain technology and IoT has the potential to revolutionize various aspects of the tourism and hospitality industry. Blockchain can provide a secure and efficient platform for managing IoT devices, enabling businesses to collect and analyze data from sensors, smart locks, and other connected devices. This integration can lead to enhanced customer experiences, improved operational efficiency, and the development of innovative services tailored to individual traveler preferences.
- *Cross-industry collaboration and interoperability*: As more businesses in the tourism and hospitality sector embrace blockchain technology, there is likely to be increased emphasis on cross-industry collaboration and interoperability. Standardization of blockchain protocols and the development of open-source platforms can facilitate seamless interactions between different businesses and services, creating a more connected and efficient ecosystem for the industry.
- *Sustainable and responsible tourism initiatives*: Blockchain technology can play a crucial role in promoting sustainable and responsible tourism practices. By providing transparent and tamper-proof records of supply chain data, environmental impacts, and other sustainability-related information, blockchain can help businesses and travelers make more informed decisions that support ethical and eco-friendly practices.
- *Tokenization of assets and services*: Tokenization refers to the process of representing real-world assets or services with digital tokens on a blockchain platform. In the context of tourism and hospitality, tokenization can enable

innovative business models, such as fractional ownership of vacation properties, or the creation of digital currencies that can be used for transactions within specific travel destinations or ecosystems.

- *Privacy-enhancing technologies*: As concerns about data privacy and protection continue to grow, the integration of privacy-enhancing technologies with blockchain platforms may become increasingly important in the tourism and hospitality industry. Techniques such as zero-knowledge proofs, confidential transactions, and encrypted data storage can help ensure that sensitive customer information remains private and secure while still enabling businesses to harness the benefits of blockchain technology.
- *Emergence of decentralized autonomous organizations (DAOs)*: DAOs are organizations that operate through self-executing rules encoded on a blockchain platform. In the tourism and hospitality sector, the emergence of DAOs could lead to new organizational structures and business models that leverage the power of decentralized decision-making and governance.

In conclusion, the potential future developments in the intersection of blockchain and tourism are vast and varied. As the technology continues to evolve and mature, it is essential for academics, industry professionals, and policymakers to stay abreast of emerging trends and innovations. By fostering collaboration and knowledge-sharing, stakeholders in the tourism and hospitality sector can harness the potential of blockchain technology to drive sustainable growth and innovation in the industry.

Preparing for the Blockchain Revolution in Tourism and Hospitality Industry

As blockchain technology continues to gain momentum and demonstrate its potential to transform the tourism and hospitality sector, it is essential for industry professionals, businesses, and policymakers to prepare for the blockchain revolution. This section outlines some of the key considerations and strategies that stakeholders can employ to ensure they are well-positioned to harness the benefits of this emerging technology. A crucial first step in preparing for the blockchain revolution is investing in education and training for industry professionals. By fostering a deeper understanding of blockchain technology, its applications, and potential challenges, businesses can make more informed decisions about adopting and integrating blockchain solutions into their operations.

The development and implementation of blockchain technology in the tourism and hospitality sector will require collaboration between various stakeholders, including businesses, technology providers, academia, and government agencies. Establishing partnerships and fostering a collaborative ecosystem can facilitate knowledge-sharing, accelerate innovation, and ensure that the industry's blockchain initiatives are aligned with broader strategic objectives. Given the evolving regulatory landscape surrounding blockchain technology, it is essential for industry stakeholders to engage with policymakers and regulators. By actively participating in discussions and providing feedback on proposed regulations, businesses can help shape policies that support innovation and growth while addressing potential risks and concerns.

To fully grasp the potential benefits and challenges of blockchain technology, businesses in the tourism and hospitality sector should consider launching pilot projects and experiments. This approach can provide valuable insights into the practical aspects of implementing blockchain solutions, helping businesses to identify potential limitations, assess the return on investment, and develop strategies for scaling their initiatives. As the blockchain revolution unfolds, businesses need to develop a long-term strategy that outlines their objectives, priorities, and action plans for harnessing the potential of this technology. This strategy should consider factors such as resource allocation, risk management, and the alignment of blockchain initiatives with broader business goals and objectives.

The blockchain revolution in tourism and hospitality is likely to be accompanied by the emergence of new trends and technologies, such as the IoTs, artificial intelligence, and virtual reality. To remain competitive and capitalize on the opportunities presented by these innovations, businesses must be agile and adaptable, continuously monitoring developments and adjusting their strategies as needed. In summary, preparing for the blockchain revolution in tourism and hospitality requires a proactive and forward-looking approach that encompasses education, collaboration, regulatory engagement, experimentation, and strategic planning. By taking these steps, industry stakeholders can ensure they are well-positioned to seize the opportunities presented by blockchain technology and drive innovation and growth in the dynamic tourism and hospitality sector.

Conclusion

To capitalize on the transformative potential of blockchain technology and drive a brighter future for the tourism and hospitality industry, businesses and stakeholders must embrace change and innovation. This involves adopting a forward-looking and proactive approach, focusing on the following key areas:

Developing a culture of innovation: Fostering a culture of innovation and openness to change is crucial for businesses seeking to harness the potential of blockchain and other emerging technologies. Encouraging experimentation, learning, and adaptation can help organizations stay ahead of the curve and remain competitive in the rapidly evolving industry landscape.

Investing in education and training: To effectively leverage the benefits of blockchain technology, businesses must invest in education and training for their employees. This will ensure that industry professionals possess the knowledge and skills required to navigate the complexities of blockchain and implement innovative solutions.

Forming strategic partnerships and collaborations: By forging strategic partnerships with technology providers, academia, and other industry stakeholders, businesses can pool resources, share knowledge, and accelerate the development and adoption of blockchain-based solutions.

Participating in policy discussions and regulation: Engaging with policymakers and regulators can help businesses contribute to the development of a supportive and conducive regulatory environment for blockchain technology in the tourism and hospitality industry.

Adapting to emerging trends and technologies: In addition to embracing blockchain technology, businesses must also stay abreast of other emerging trends and technologies, such as artificial intelligence, virtual reality, and the IoTs. By maintaining an adaptive and agile approach, organizations can capitalize on new opportunities and drive innovation across the tourism and hospitality sector.

In conclusion, embracing change and innovation is vital for harnessing the transformative potential of blockchain technology and ensuring a brighter future for the tourism and hospitality industry. As the industry continues to evolve and adapt to the changing needs of travelers, embracing cutting-edge technologies like blockchain will be critical for ensuring long-term success and competitiveness in the dynamic tourism and hospitality sector.

References

Dogru, T., Mody, M., & Leonardi, C. (2018). Blockchain technology & its implications for the hospitality industry. *Boston Hospitality Review*. Boston University School of Hospitality Administration.

Iansiti, M., & Lakhani, K. R. (2017). The truth about blockchain. *Harvard Business Review*. Retreived April 10, 2018 from https://hbr.org/2017/01/the-truth-about-blockchain.

Onder, I., & Treiblmaier, H. (2018). Blockchain and tourism: Three research propositions. *Annals of Tourism Research, 72*(C), 180–182.

Pedak, M. (2018). The effect of tourism on GDP. Bachelor's Thesis. Jönköping University, Jonkoping, Sweden.

Windingtree. (2020). Overview. Retrieved on February 14, 2020 from https://developers.windingtree.com/.

3

EXPLORING BLOCKCHAIN IN FOOD AND AGRICULTURAL SUPPLY CHAINS

Tolga Benli, Ismail Erol, İ. Tolga Medeni, Tunç Medeni, and Muhiba Ahmed Khan

Introduction

Supply chains, as a network of several entities, create value for consumers and their associated activities through collaboration. In today's global market, consumers are the most important factors affecting supply chain decision processes, and supply chain management is essential to achieving them. A well-functioning supply chain will create value for all stakeholders as well as meet the needs of consumers (Thomas & Griffin, 1996). A successful supply chain management process will make material flows, money transfers, and information sharing as efficient and effective as possible. It also plays a key role in the competitive environment between companies (Lambert & Cooper, 2000). Thus, supply chains will become innovative to adapt to increasing competition.

The food and agricultural supply chains (F&ASCs) also include several operations beginning with the supply of quality and safe raw materials, processing the food, distributing intermediate and finished products, and reaching the consumer (Aung & Chang, 2014). As in all supply chains, F&ASCs have certain requirements to create an effective structure. Criteria such as providing effective logistics management, ensuring information flow among stakeholders, and adapting to changes in standards are significant for F&ASCs (Stranieri et al., 2021). Food safety is another prominent factor, especially due to the increase in food-related health problems. Risks to human health, limited shelf life, delicate quality, and other factors differentiate the food production industry from other industries. To address these factors, F&ASCs must be both transparent and visible, which are the most significant features of a supply chain (George et al., 2019; Longo et al., 2020; Peng et al., 2022).

It is argued that disruptive technologies, including artificial intelligence, blockchain, 3D manufacturing, the internet of things, and radio frequency identification,

DOI: 10.4324/9781003351917-3

are employed to ensure improved transparency and traceability (Bhat et al., 2022; Kamilaris et al., 2019; Wang et al., 2022).

Out of these emerging innovations, blockchain technology (BcT) has grown in significance. Blockchain, also referred to as distributed ledger technology, is a method of encrypting data in a network environment before it is saved in an immutable distributed database and simultaneously viewed by all users (Demestichas et al., 2020; Dey & Shekhawat, 2021; Lin et al., 2017). Through its features, BcT can address various challenges to supply chains. Using BcT, documents are stored in chronological order in "blocks." Hence, BcT provides high levels of security and are difficult to falsify (Bai et al., 2022; Pranto et al., 2021).

F&ASCs also have certain challenges, including uncertainties in quality, a lack of data and information, difficulty in calculating environmental damage, imbalances in supply and demand, delays in processes due to the high number of intermediaries, high intermediary costs, and a lack of trust among stakeholders. It is suggested that BcT has potential to alleviate the impact of these challenges through improved security, transparency, traceability, efficiency, speed, and automation. The goal of this chapter is to review the current state of the art and present several future research opportunities on blockchain-based F&ASCs.

This study will seek answers to the following research questions:

RQ_1: What are the problems in F&ASCs based on the existing literature?
RQ_2: How can the problems in F&ASCs be resolved using BcT?
RQ_3: What methods are used in the current state of the art, and how can they be categorized?
RQ_4: What could be the future research opportunities with respect to BcT in F&ASCs?

The rest of this chapter is structured as follows: the background of the topic is provided in Section "Background." In Section "Literature Review," the literature review as well as the data collection and search strategy are presented. Discussion is introduced in Section "Discussion." Finally in Section "Conclusions," conclusions and suggestions for future research are presented.

Background

Blockchain Technology

Since it originally appeared in the Bitcoin white paper, BcT has grown out of the creation of the virtual currency known as Bitcoin (Nakamoto, 2008). Blockchain is a distributed database of records that is executed and shared among participating entities. The foundation of BcT, also known as disrupted ledger technology, is an immutable online ledger that has begun to transcend numerous operational services, commercial transactions, and technological practices of many businesses around the world (Zheng et al., 2017). Rather than being stored in a single location, ledgers in BcT are dispersed throughout the network, enabling users to have access, which is more secure, persistent, auditable, anonymous, and decentralized (Nam et al., 2021). In a blockchain, all blocks share a comparable timestamp. Simply put, transactions are controlled by grouping them into blocks. Each block contains a hash of the one before it, and network nodes preferentially connect the blocks in chronological order. Hence, an architecture in blockchain is successful in upholding a trustworthy and auditable registry for all linked transactions (Alshamsi et al., 2022). Smart contracts, which are digital contracts that take effect automatically when certain conditions are met, are another feature of blockchain. Smart contacts can boost trust and greatly speed up transactions across supply chains. Compared to the traditional methods, they reduce paperwork, expedite processing, and minimize human effort (Duan et al., 2020; López-Pimentel et al., 2022; Zhang & Kim, 2022).

In addition, BcT can allow supply chains to reduce the number of intermediary organizations, and with its highly secured decentralized structure, BcT ensures business transactions in a real-time manner, which will improve the effectiveness of supply chains (Chaganti et al., 2022; Kamble et al., 2020). A representation of a blockchain-based transaction is demonstrated in Figure 3.1.

Some of the benefits of BcT include increased security, better transparency, real-time traceability, improved efficiency and speed, and automation. BcT can also be used to address various problems that F&ASCs have. The following section discusses F&ASCs and how BcT is employed to address certain challenges faced across F&ASCs.

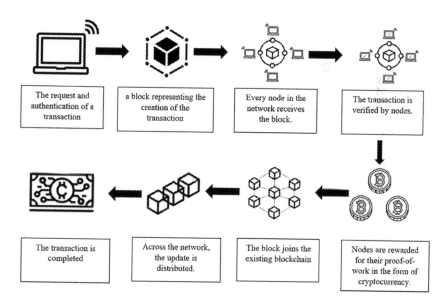

The request and authentication of a transaction

a block representing the creation of the transaction

Every node in the network receives the block.

The transaction is verified by nodes.

The transaction is completed

Across the network, the update is distributed.

The block joins the existing blockchain

Nodes are rewarded for their proof-of-work in the form of cryptocurrency.

FIGURE 3.1   How blockchain works.

Blockchain in Food and Agriculture Supply Chains

F&ASCs demonstrated in Figure 3.2 involve multiple stakeholders, including farmers, shipping companies, wholesalers, retailers, distributors, and groceries. Starting with the seed, the procedures of harvesting the farm's raw materials, converting the intermediate product into the finished product in the production facility, transporting and distributing the finished product, and finally taking its place on the market shelves are outlined in Figure 3.2.

These activities should be assumed collaboratively to create maximum value. Because there are more stakeholders and outside forces at play in F&ASCs than in other supply chains, F&ASCs are more complicated and challenging to manage. Additionally, the shelf life of agri-food products is limited (Tharatipyakul and Pongnumkul, 2021). By providing the supply chain partners with accurate information at the right time, the collaborative effort could be facilitated (Khan et al., 2022b). The current F&ASCs also need to meet the nutritional needs of a growing population, reduce environmental footprint, promote more sustainable agriculture methods, improve food safety, and reduce supply chain costs (Niknejad et al., 2021; Khan et al., 2022a).

It is argued that ensuring food safety calls for enhanced traceability. It is also argued that as information is shared and particular tasks are assigned to various supply chain stakeholders, traceability increases (Garaus and Treiblmaier, 2021). In other words, addressing compliance with food safety and sustainability standards requires improved transparency by keeping track of every aspect of F&ASC operations. Besides traceability, trust is an important factor in F&ASCs. Smart contracts will provide a tool to respond to both issues. More specifically, BcT-based smart contracts will help reduce costs by reducing the number of financial institutions. Besides smart contracts, other technologies such as big data, artificial intelligence, cloud-based system, and RFID can be integrated into BcT to improve supply chain bottom line (Burgess et al., 2022).

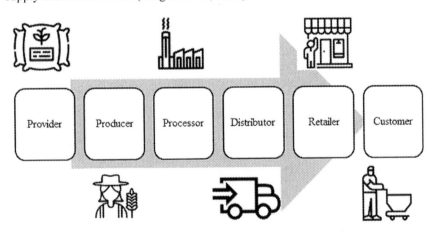

FIGURE 3.2   Food and agriculture supply chain.

In summary, BcT can provide the following benefits for A&FSCs: (1) data can be calibrated from multiple supply chains concurrently (Dayana and Kalpana, 2021), (2) the entire journey of products through a supply chain can be tracked (Kamilaris et al., 2019; Krithika, 2022), (3) lead times will be shortened because the processes will move more quickly (Kamble et al., 2020; Stranieri et al., 2021), (4) productivity will be improved, and supply chains will be more robust and resilient (Mangla et al., 2022; Sharma et al., 2022), and (5) enhanced security will be ensured using smart contracts (Bai et al., 2022; Chaganti et al., 2022).

Literature Review

The literature search in this study was conducted utilizing the Web of Science (WoS) databases. For publications in all domains, the search terms "blockchain" AND "supply chain" AND "food and agriculture" were used. A total of 51 papers on blockchain-based F&ASCs are considered for review, excluding books and book chapters, editorials, and conference proceedings. The language of the selected articles is English. The existing studies published before 2020 were not included since they were already demonstrated in most of the existing review studies. Table 3.1 summarizes the recent state of the art.

TABLE 3.1 Summary of the literature review

Reference	Method	Goal	Key contribution
Xiong et al. (2020)	Conceptual	To examine the theoretical and practical uses of BcT in the agriculture industry, including transactions for agricultural products, insurance for farmers, and smart farming.	Explaining the potential applications and limitations of BcT in F&ASCs through a systematic review.
Bumblauskas et al. (2020)	Use case analysis	To explain how companies are using BcT to improve the production and transportation of eggs from farm to customer.	Using a systematic use case analysis to investigate whether BcT can benefit the food business and provide evidence that it can improve food traceability.

(Continued)

TABLE 3.1 (Continued)

Reference	Method	Goal	Key contribution
Longo et al. (2020)	Literature review	To review the existing studies on how BcT can impact the cost of each operation in the supply chain from dairy farms to end-users.	Reviewing the state of the art systematically and proposing a possible design alternative for the relevant data to be stored on the Ethereum blockchain.
Chen et al. (2020)	Case study	To make a definition of the term "digital agricultural democratization" to reflect the interconnectedness of technical logic and institutional logic.	Demonstrating a case study to address issues such as asymmetric information, trusted third-party agencies, and insufficient traceability of organic food.
Kamble et al. (2020)	MCDM	To identify and relate factors that support BcT adoption in the F&ASCs.	Developing an MCDM framework to show the factors that boost food safety in F&ASCs.
Ferrag et al. (2020)	Survey-based empirical study	To summarize research issues related to security and privacy in the context of IoT-based green farming.	Reviewing the challenges systematically to discuss the potential future research directions in the security and privacy of green IoT-based agriculture.
Torky and Hassanein (2020)	Survey-based empirical study	To review smart applications for precision agriculture that integrates blockchain with IoT.	Proposing innovative blockchain-IoT-based business models as vital solutions to important problems related to the precision farming systems.
Demestichas et al. (2020)	Literature review	To provide an overview of how BcT is used to ensure traceability in the agri-food industry.	Reviewing the existing state of the art analytically to discuss the relevant business practices that already exist, highlight the associated challenges, and outline the potential future uses of blockchain technologies in the agri-food supply chain.

(Continued)

TABLE 3.1 (Continued)

Reference	Method	Goal	Key contribution
van Hilten et al. (2020)	Case study	To clarify the challenges that BcT-based organic food supply chains must address.	Using a case study that shows the successful implementation of whole chain traceability for organic and fair-trade foods. Hence, providing a platform for future work on regulations governing food traceability in the European Union would be possible.
Duan et al. (2020)	Literature review	To review the literature on the use of blockchain in the food supply chain.	Using a content analysis methodology to review the existing studies on BcT in food supply chains.
Motta et al. (2020)	Case study	To scrutinize possible applications of blockchain in the agri-food industry using a case study methodology focused on early adopters.	Examining the blockchain applications in the agri-food supply chain using case studies to address and overcome issues with trust and transparency.
Ali et al. (2021)	Case study	To suggest a sustainable blockchain framework in the halal food supply chain.	Implementing blockchain in the halal food supply chain to overcome major challenges, including economies of scale, risk of incompatibility, employee resistance to change, and overlapping meta-system.
van Wassenaer et al. (2021)	Use case analysis	To provide an overview of the decisions that need to be made at the ledger, governance structure, and ecosystem layers of a blockchain application.	Providing a systematic overview of the choices that need to be made in the stages of a blockchain implementation, and providing a framework for understanding various blockchain applications.

(Continued)

TABLE 3.1 (Continued)

Reference	Method	Goal	Key contribution
Dayana and Kalpana (2021)	Survey-based empirical study	To explore the effect of BcT on food supply chains.	Discussing the applicability of BcT for more transparent food supply chains.
Dey and Shekhawat (2021)	Use case analysis	To discuss how integrating blockchain with IoT can improve IoT network performance in agricultural value chains.	Exploring the concept of e-farm through benefit sharing, enhanced coordination between actors in the value chain, and real-time decision making.
Garaus and Treiblmaier (2021)	Conceptual	To assess how the traceability of food products affects consumers' trust in the store, and then how it influences consumers' choice of retailer.	Indicating how less well-known retailers benefit from BcT than better-known retailers in terms of boosting consumer confidence. Indicating also educating consumers about blockchain advantages reinforces the benefits of a blockchain-based traceability system.
Nayal et al. (2021)	Survey-based empirical study	To investigate the current state of the art to explore how the adoption of BcT affects the effectiveness of sustainable supply chains.	Helping better understand the variables affecting BcT and how BcT can increase the efficiency of sustainable supply chains.
Kramer et al. (2021)	Literature review	To examine how the use of various types of BcT platforms affects coordination mechanisms in vertically cooperative agri-food networks.	Revealing that the choice of a particular agri-food network, coordination mechanisms, and digital business model used are important for effectively managing the supply chain network.
Niknejad et al. (2021)	Literature review	To review the current studies on BcT with a focus on food and agriculture disciplines.	Showing how food and agriculture studies on BcT are categorized.

(Continued)

TABLE 3.1 (Continued)

Reference	Method	Goal	Key contribution
Pranto et al. (2021)	Blockchain-based model	To explore various applications of BcT and smart contracts with the inclusion of IoT devices in the pre-harvest and post-harvest stages of agriculture.	Demonstrating the immutable, accessible, transparent, and robustly secure features of blockchain in the context of agriculture while at the same time highlighting the robust mechanism offered by the combination of blockchain, smart contracts, and IoT.
Tharatipyakul and Pongnumkul (2021)	Literature review	To review the existing studies of BcT on food quality and safety.	Discovering the blockchain applications using a systematic review.
Sengupta and Kim (2021)	Conceptual	To summarize how BcT is used in Canada's A&FSCs.	Providing suggestions on how to implement BcT in A&FSCs.
Alobid et al. (2022)	Literature review	To discuss existing studies of BcT in agriculture industry.	Reviewing existing research, with particular attention paid to the current state of the art on BcT in agriculture, its associated problems, and its future significance by various nations.
Bai et al. (2022)	MCDM (multicriteria decision making)	To improve sustainable supply chain transparency by developing a BcT-based hierarchical enablers framework in the cocoa industry.	Ensuring the measurement of blockchain-based sustainable supply chain transparency enablers in the context of emerging African economies.
Bhat et al. (2022)	Conceptual	To address the scalability, interoperability, security, privacy, and storage concerns in BcT-based F&ASCs.	Demonstrating use cases of various acting entities throughout the supply chain to indicate their improved performance.

(*Continued*)

TABLE 3.1 (Continued)

Reference	Method	Goal	Key contribution
Burgess et al. (2022)	Literature review	To propose a blockchain-based quality management architecture in food supply chains.	Proposing a blockchain network to improve supply chain quality control in food supply chains.
Chaganti et al. (2022)	Blockchain-based model	To propose a framework to mitigate the impact of behavioral pattern-based security attacks by anomaly monitoring.	Identifying security irregularities and warning farm nodes in a real-time manner.
Dasaklis et al. (2022)	Literature review	To review the F&ASCs traceability systems enabled by blockchain.	Offering key conclusions regarding the unresolved problems and difficulties of current blockchain traceability implementations as well as promising areas for future study. Developing and testing real-world traceability solutions with respect to cost and sustainability.
David et al. (2022)	Survey-based empirical study	To explain how BCT can be used to organize the food industry.	Explaining the biggest benefits and weaknesses of BcT in F&ASCs.
Khan et al. (2022a)	Interview	To examine the use of BcT in agricultural supply chains during the COVID-19 pandemic.	Showing that practitioners can use BcT to manage agricultural supply chains during pandemics such as COVID-19.
Khan et al. (2022b)	Literature review	To identify and examine the obstacles to the adoption of blockchain in the food supply chain.	Focusing on how BcT can be used effectively in the food supply chains of the emerging economies.

(Continued)

TABLE 3.1 (Continued)

Reference	Method	Goal	Key contribution
Krithika (2022)	Survey-based empirical study	To review the literature on how blockchain has benefited and will continue to benefit various market segments in agriculture.	Showing how BcT is expected to have a major impact on the agricultural sector and several related sectors in the future.
Krzyzanowski Guerra and Boys (2022)	Conceptual	To review the laws and regulations with respect to BcT in F&ASCs.	Discussing how the US agri-food system could be affected by the current regulatory approach to blockchain adoption.
Mangla et al. (2022)	MCDM	To create a BcT-based sustainable tea supply chain.	Proposing a systematic framework to build a BcT-based sustainable tea supply chain.
Pandey et al. (2022)	Literature review	To demonstrate the immense scope and importance of BcT in food supply chains.	Presenting an overview of blockchain usage in food supply chains as well as a discussion of adoption issues including scalability, interoperability, and high cost.
Panghal et al. (2022)	MCDM	To identify the challenges in implementing BcT in food supply chains of India.	Proposing a decision framework to explore the challenges to adopting BcT.
Peng et al. (2022)	Blockchain-based model	To suggest a model to ensure the safety and quality of rice.	Proposing a novel paradigm by incorporating the theories and techniques of BcT into the agricultural research.
Sendros et al. (2022)	Literature review	To review the studies that identify the agricultural operations that use BcT.	Conducting a scoping review that uses a formal systematic literature review methodology and answers open-ended research questions.

(*Continued*)

TABLE 3.1 (Continued)

Reference	Method	Goal	Key contribution
Sharma et al. (2022)	MCDM	To identify what enablers and obstacles to BCT adoption stand out in the agricultural supply chains.	Proposing an MCDM framework to discover the differences in facilitating factors between various economies for BCT adoption in the agricultural supply chain.
Singh and Raza (2022)	Conceptual	To review the studies on how to automate the food chain management system.	Showing the potential solutions based on the integration of IoT and BCT via literature review.
Talha Talukder et al. (2022)	Case study	To propose a food delivery system based on blockchain and smart contracts to address issues such as information security, business-to-business competition, and strict policy enforcement.	Suggesting a food delivery system that uses smart contracts to address certain problems.
Tan et al. (2022)	Case study	To identify the current traceability issues that Malaysia's food supply chain is facing to meet halal regulations.	Proposing a conceptual framework incorporating halal procedures and technology with input from three blockchain software vendors to increase the traceability of the farm-to-table halal food supply chain.
Trollman et al. (2022)	Case study	To identify how BcT can help improve the coffee supply chain performance.	Reviewing the existing literature systematically to exhibit how BcT is used to address the problem of waste throughout the supply chain.

(Continued)

TABLE 3.1 (Continued)

Reference	Method	Goal	Key contribution
Vu et al. (2022)	Interview	To create a fact-backed blockchain application model for the food industry.	Developing an empirically validated application model that provides a comprehensive roadmap for launching blockchain projects in food supply chains.
Wang et al. (2022)	Case study	To integrate RFID with BcT to create a foundation for a supply chain traceability system.	Developing a BcT-based RFID system to facilitate product tracking.
Zhang et al. (2022)	Conceptual	To highlight the benefits of blockchain in the existing fresh fruit supply chain.	Discussing conceptually to exhibit how IoT and BcT gather and upload reliable data from fruit picking to final consumption in fresh fruit supply chains.
Zhang and Kim (2022)	Case study	To discuss a case on smart contracts to increase the reliability of restaurant reviews.	Proposing a peer-to-peer BcT-based framework.
Zhou et al. (2022)	Conceptual	To discuss disruptive technologies and their uses in food safety.	Systematically discussing the future issues with respect to the uses of artificial intelligence, big data, and BcT in food safety practices.
Zkik et al. (2022)	MCDM	To examine the adoption of BcT for sustainability in supply chains for e-enabled agriculture, along with the barriers to its adoption.	Developing an MCDM framework to measure the sustainability performance of BcT-based agricultural supply chain.
Cricelli et al. (2023)	Literature review	To examine the ways in which various agri-food supply chains can seize opportunities and respond to the challenges after the COVID-19 pandemic.	Highlighting the characteristics of supply chains and discussing how successfully Industry 4.0 technologies have been adopted in the agri-food supply chains.

(Continued)

TABLE 3.1 (Continued)

Reference	Method	Goal	Key contribution
Pakseresht et al. (2023)	Literature review	To review the existing studies that discuss the contribution of BcT to the transition to a better circular food system.	Providing insights for supply chain managers that seek to achieve the transition to the circular economy as well as recommendations for future research areas.

As shown in Table 3.1, a classification framework is used in this review to better understand the existing studies on blockchain-based F&ASCs. The studies are classified according to their methods, goals, and key contributions. Note that certain concepts stand out more than the others. Although food safety, food quality, and food traceability issues are common, the challenges to the adoption of blockchain in F&SCSs and the benefits of blockchain for supply chains are widely studied. In addition, the integration of BcT with other disruptive technologies (IoT, RFID, etc.) to create more sustainable F&ASCs has been extensively addressed.

Discussion

In this section, four research questions are addressed based on the literature review. Since the journey of the product through F&ASCs is not transparent enough, there is uncertainty in terms of quality. More specifically, due to the insufficiency in data and information, uncertainties occur in measuring the environmental impact of manufacturing processes (Stranieri et al., 2021). It is also challenging to record changes in logistics processes in real time. Simply put, insufficient supply and demand data will result in overstock or stock-out. Similarly, the uncertainty of the origin and authenticity of the product will cause customers to have minimal knowledge about a supply chain (Nam et al., 2021). Although supply chain management is a key tool that helps address food insecurity and contributes to public health problems, in a complex supply chain such as food and agriculture, it will be difficult to ensure efficient traceability. Thus, food recall may not be possible, and there may be significant harm to public health (Duan et al., 2020). When evaluated in terms of the dimensions of sustainability (economic, social, and environmental), traditional supply chains can be ineffective at many points. Ineffectiveness in transparency, traceability, and efficiency of the operations involved in F&ASCs will wreak havoc on business reputation and supply chain sustainability (Bhat et al., 2022; Mangla et al., 2022). Hence, RQ_1 is answered.

It is argued that blockchain-based supply chains have some advantages over traditional supply chains. In general, immutability, decentralization, consensus mechanisms, traceability, security, and auditability are some of the main issues in supply chain processes that BcT helps to address (Nam et al., 2021; Nayal et al.,

2021; Sharma et al., 2022). For example, using smart contracts, the supply chain's ability to control quality will be facilitated by removing the need for intermediary institutions (David et al., 2022; Kamilaris et al., 2019; Pranto et al., 2021). A BcT-based platform establishes a new digital institution of trust to reduce buyer and seller uncertainty and improve the efficiency, transparency, and traceability of the flow of value and information, which is essential to the F&ASCs and broader global economy (Tripoli and Schmidhuber, 2018).

In addition, logistics processes and stock management will be achieved using real-time data. Hence, it will be possible to mitigate the negative effects of changes on supply and demand (Dey and Shekhawat, 2021). Due to improved transparency, customers will make more informed purchasing decisions. Being able to track products throughout the supply chain will provide decision makers with the opportunity to respond to the food safety emergencies in a short time (Hastig and Sodhi, 2020; Pakseresht et al., 2023). Another challenge in F&ASCs that BcT may address is with respect to small producers. Nowadays, sustainability increases its importance for stakeholders. However, small producers cannot perform such activities due to their high costs (George et al., 2019). It is suggested that costs may decrease since BcT simplifies the operations across F&ASCs.

Lastly, thanks to smart contracts, it will be possible to eliminate paperwork, and hence the credit and debt turnover of small producers will increase. In addition, when technology-enabled transparency provides accurate and quick solutions for controlling foodborne illness outbreaks, a considerable decrease in healthcare expenditures and improvements in the public's opinion of F&ASCs can be ensured (Astill et al., 2019). Hence, RQ_2 are responded. Answers to RQ_1 and RQ_2 are summarized in Table 3.2.

TABLE 3.2 Problems in F&ASCs and possible blockchain-based solutions

Problems	Possible solutions
Uncertainties in quality Lack of data and information	Providing full transparency, all network participants with permissioned access see the same information simultaneously
Lack of having a method to measure environmental impacts	Thanks to its high traceability, every process that is harmful to the environment can be monitored instantly
Real-time recording of logistics activities	With the possibility of adding transactions to the block instantly, every stage in logistics can be tracked
Imbalance in supply and demand	Making predictions becomes easier as information and data are easily accessible to all stakeholders on a blockchain-based network
Delays in processes due to the high number of intermediaries High intermediary costs	Smart contracts can eliminate intermediaries and reduce intermediary costs
Lack of trust among stakeholders	BcT ensures immutability

This part of the discussion answers RQ_3. Based on the literature review in this study, 51 articles were selected and clustered according to their methods in Figure 3.3. In general, as shown in Figure 3.3, the methods used in these studies were clustered in eight separate groups.

Out of the existing studies, note that most of the papers are based on literature reviews. Figure 3.3 also indicates that the conceptual studies are ranked second. Note also that future studies may be more diverse due to the rising popularity of the topic. Our literature review suggests that blockchain applications in F&ASCs are still in its early stages. Hence, there are several research opportunities on the potential challenges that may be faced during blockchain implementations. The potential research opportunities are shown in Table 3.3, which provides an answer to RQ_4.

As indicated in Table 3.3, there are many different types of research gaps that researchers may wish to consider since BcT is still in its infancy. For example, new studies are needed to improve the technical features of BcT on interoperability, scalability, security, and privacy. Another vital area of research is about the legislative issues and regulations that help blockchain to be implemented effectively. Specifically, researchers must perform studies on how new blockchain-related regulations should be written. Next, new research about the critical success factors, barriers, enablers, and organizational policies of blockchain-based F&ASCS must be conducted. The components of a supply chain or project that are crucial to its success are known as critical success factors or enablers. To keep a supply chain

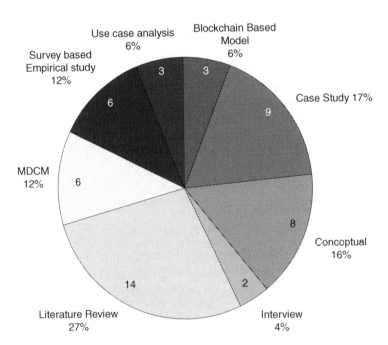

FIGURE 3.3 Percentage of reviewed articles by methods.

TABLE 3.3 Future research opportunities

Future research opportunities
1   Complexity in blockchain-based F&ASCs
2   Operating cost in blockchain-based F&ASCs
3   Long-term impacts of BcT on F&ASCs
4   User interfaces for incorporating users into system evaluation and development
5   Challenges to BcT that F&ASCs must deal with
6   Identifying which farms would suffer and which would benefit from the implementation of blockchain in F&ASCs
7   Standardization of blockchain-based F&ASCs
8   Discover how the technology can be used to improve environmental performance in agri-food businesses
9   Government roles and functions in BcT-based F&ASCs
10   Interoperability of blockchain platforms
11   Legal issues and regulations
12   Enablers and critical success factors for implementing BcT in F&ASCs effectively
13   Case studies on incorporating BcT with other disruptive technologies

or project focused on what needs to be done to succeed, it is crucial to identify and communicate critical success factors throughout the supply chain.

Last but not the least, new case studies that explore how BcT is implemented across F&ASCs should also be published. Note that these application examples provide invaluable insights for practitioners.

Conclusions

F&ASCs face several challenges encountered in the process of turning raw materials into products on the shelf. Researchers suggest that one of the technologies that can be used to overcome these challenges is BcT. The goal of this study is to review the literature on the use of BcT in F&ASCs. To achieve that, using specific keywords, 51 journal articles published between 2020 and 2023 were reviewed using the WoS database.

In this study, four research questions were addressed. Note that there are several challenges associated with the traditional F&ASCs, including traceability, food safety, information sharing between stakeholders, transparency, and logistics management. It is argued that the main reason for these problems is the uncertainties arising from the lack of information and data. The existing research also suggests that BcT has the potential to improve traceability, security, trust, and transparency throughout F&ASCs through its functions, and there are various research opportunities that researchers should address in their future studies. Since BcT is still a new concept, it might take some time for BcT to fully streamline F&ASCs around the world on a larger scale.

This review chapter also has certain limitations despite its contributions. For example, it excludes the existing book chapters, conference proceedings, master theses, and PhD dissertations. Future review studies are needed to consider those researches to address BcT in F&ASCs more comprehensively.

References

Ali, M. H., Chung, L., Kumar, A., Zailani, S., & Tan, K. H. (2021). A sustainable Blockchain framework for the halal food supply chain: Lessons from Malaysia. *Technological Forecasting and Social Change*, *170*(120870). https://doi.org/10.1016/j.techfore.2021.120870.

Alobid, M., Abujudeh, S., & Szűcs, I. (2022). The role of blockchain in revolutionizing the agricultural sector. *Sustainability (Switzerland)*, *14*(7), 1–15. https://doi.org/10.3390/su14074313.

Alshamsi, M., Al-Emran, M., & Shaalan, K. (2022). A systematic review on blockchain adoption. *Applied Sciences (Switzerland)*, *12*(9), 1–18. https://doi.org/10.3390/app12094245.

Astill, J., Dara, R. A., Campbell, M., Farber, J. M., Fraser, E. D. G., Sharif, S., & Yada, R. Y. (2019). Transparency in food supply chains: A review of enabling technology solutions. *Trends in Food Science and Technology*, *91*(December 2018), 240–247. https://doi.org/10.1016/j.tifs.2019.07.024.

Aung, M. M., & Chang, Y. S. (2014). Traceability in a food supply chain: Safety and quality perspectives. *Food Control*, *39*(1), 172–184. https://doi.org/10.1016/j.foodcont.2013.11.007.

Bai, C., Quayson, M., & Sarkis, J. (2022). Analysis of blockchain's enablers for improving sustainable supply chain transparency in Africa cocoa industry. *Journal of Cleaner Production*, *358*(October 2020), 131896. https://doi.org/10.1016/j.jclepro.2022.131896.

Bhat, S. A., Huang, N. F., Sofi, I. B., & Sultan, M. (2022). Agriculture-food supply chain management based on blockchain and IoT: A narrative on enterprise blockchain interoperability. *Agriculture (Switzerland)*, *12*(1). https://doi.org/10.3390/agriculture12010040.

Bumblauskas, D., Mann, A., Dugan, B., & Rittmer, J. (2020). A blockchain use case in food distribution: Do you know where your food has been? *International Journal of Information Management*, *52*(March 2019), 102008. https://doi.org/10.1016/j.ijinfomgt.2019.09.004.

Burgess, P., Sunmola, F., & Wertheim-Heck, S. (2022). Blockchain enabled quality management in short food supply chains. *Procedia Computer Science*, *200*(2019), 904–913. https://doi.org/10.1016/j.procs.2022.01.288.

Chaganti, R., Varadarajan, V., Gorantla, V. S., Gadekallu, T. R., & Ravi, V. (2022). Blockchain-based cloud-enabled security monitoring using internet of things in smart agriculture. *Future Internet*, *14*(9), 1–20. https://doi.org/10.3390/fi14090250.

Chen, Y., Li, Y., & Li, C. (2020). Electronic agriculture, blockchain and digital agricultural democratization: Origin, theory and application. *Journal of Cleaner Production*, *268*. https://doi.org/10.1016/j.jclepro.2020.122071.

Cricelli, L., Mauriello, R., & Strazzullo, S. (2023). Technological innovation in agri-food supply chains. *British Food Journal*, *ahead-of-p* (ahead-of-print). https://doi.org/10.1108/BFJ-06-2022-0490.

Dasaklis, T. K., Voutsinas, T. G., Tsoulfas, G. T., & Casino, F. (2022). A systematic literature review of blockchain-enabled supply chain traceability implementations. *Sustainability (Switzerland)*, *14*(4), 1–30. https://doi.org/10.3390/su14042439.

David, A., Kumar, C. G., & Paul, P. V. (2022). Blockchain technology in the food supply chain: Empirical analysis. *International Journal of Information Systems and Supply Chain Management*, *15*(3), 1–12. https://doi.org/10.4018/IJISSCM.290014.

Dayana, S., & Kalpana, G. (2021). Survey on agri-food supply chain using blockchain. *Proceedings of the 5th International Conference on I-SMAC (IoT in Social, Mobile, Analytics and Cloud), I-SMAC 2021*. https://doi.org/10.1109/I-SMAC52330.2021.9640768.

Demestichas, K., Peppes, N., Alexakis, T., & Adamopoulou, E. (2020). Blockchain in agriculture traceability systems: A review. *Applied Sciences (Switzerland)*, *10*(12), 1–22. https://doi.org/10.3390/APP10124113.

Dey, K., & Shekhawat, U. (2021). Blockchain for sustainable e-agriculture: Literature review, architecture for data management, and implications. *Journal of Cleaner Production*, *316*(July), 128254. https://doi.org/10.1016/j.jclepro.2021.128254.

Duan, J., Zhang, C., Gong, Y., Brown, S., & Li, Z. (2020). A content-analysis based literature review in blockchain adoption within food supply chain. *International Journal of Environmental Research and Public Health*, *17*(5). https://doi.org/10.3390/ijerph17051784.

Ferrag, M. A., Shu, L., Yang, X., Derhab, A., & Maglaras, L. (2020). Security and privacy for green IoT-based agriculture: Review, blockchain solutions, and challenges. *IEEE Access*, *8*, 32031–32053. https://doi.org/10.1109/ACCESS.2020.2973178.

Garaus, M., & Treiblmaier, H. (2021). The influence of blockchain-based food traceability on retailer choice: The mediating role of trust. *Food Control*, *129*(December 2020), 108082. https://doi.org/10.1016/j.foodcont.2021.108082.

George, R. V., Harsh, H. O., Ray, P., & Babu, A. K. (2019). Food quality traceability prototype for restaurants using blockchain and food quality data index. *Journal of Cleaner Production*, *240*, 118021. https://doi.org/10.1016/j.jclepro.2019.118021.

Hastig, G. M., & Sodhi, M. M. S. (2020). Blockchain for supply chain traceability: Business requirements and critical success factors. *Production and Operations Management*, *29*(4), 935–954. https://doi.org/10.1111/poms.13147.

Kamble, S. S., Gunasekaran, A., & Sharma, R. (2020). Modeling the blockchain enabled traceability in agriculture supply chain. *International Journal of Information Management*, *52*(November 2018), 101967. https://doi.org/10.1016/j.ijinfomgt.2019.05.023.

Kamilaris, A., Fonts, A., & Prenafeta-Boldú, F. X. (2019). The rise of blockchain technology in agriculture and food supply chains. *Trends in Food Science and Technology*, *91*(July), 640–652. https://doi.org/10.1016/j.tifs.2019.07.034.

Khan, H. H., Malik, M. N., Konečná, Z., Chofreh, A. G., Goni, F. A., & Klemeš, J. J. (2022a). Blockchain technology for agricultural supply chains during the COVID-19 pandemic: Benefits and cleaner solutions. *Journal of Cleaner Production*, *347*(December 2021). https://doi.org/10.1016/j.jclepro.2022.131268.

Khan, S., Kaushik, M. K., Kumar, R., & Khan, W. (2022b). Investigating the barriers of blockchain technology integrated food supply chain: A BWM approach. *Benchmarking: An International Journal*, *ahead-of-p* (ahead-of-print). https://doi.org/10.1108/BIJ-08-2021-0489.

Kramer, M. P., Bitsch, L., & Hanf, J. (2021). Blockchain and its impacts on agri-food upply chain network management. *Sustainability (Switzerland)*, *13*(4), 1–22. https://doi.org/10.3390/su13042168.

Krithika, L. B. (2022). Survey on applications of blockchain in agriculture. *Agriculture*, *12*(9), 1333. https://doi.org/10.3390/agriculture12091333.

Krzyzanowski Guerra, K., & Boys, K. A. (2022). A new food chain: Adoption and policy implications to blockchain use in agri-food industries. *Applied Economic Perspectives and Policy*, *44*(1), 324–349. https://doi.org/10.1002/aepp.13163.

Lambert, D. M., & Cooper, M. C. (2000). Issues in supply chain management. *Industrial Marketing Management*, *29*(1), 65–83.

Lin, Y. P., Petway, J. R., Anthony, J., Mukhtar, H., Liao, S. W., Chou, C. F., & Ho, Y. F. (2017). Blockchain: The evolutionary next step for ICT e-agriculture. *Environments - MDPI*, *4*(3), 1–13. https://doi.org/10.3390/environments4030050.

Longo, F., Nicoletti, L., & Padovano, A. (2020). Estimating the impact of blockchain adoption in the food processing industry and supply chain. *International Journal of Food Engineering*, *16*(5–6), 1–18. https://doi.org/10.1515/ijfe-2019-0109.

López-Pimentel, J. C., Alcaraz-Rivera, M., Granillo-Macías, R., & Olivares-Benitez, E. (2022). Traceability of Mexican avocado supply chain: A microservice and blockchain technological solution. *Sustainability*, *14*(21), 14633. https://doi.org/10.3390/su142114633.

Mangla, S. K., Kazançoğlu, Y., Yıldızbaşı, A., Öztürk, C., & Çalık, A. (2022). A conceptual framework for blockchain-based sustainable supply chain and evaluating implementation barriers: A case of the tea supply chain. *Business Strategy and the Environment*, (October), 3693–3716. https://doi.org/10.1002/bse.3027.

Motta, G. A., Tekinerdogan, B., & Athanasiadis, I. N. (2020). Blockchain applications in the agri-food domain: The first wave. *Frontiers in Blockchain*, *3*(February), 1–13. https://doi.org/10.3389/fbloc.2020.00006.

Nakamoto, S. (2008). Bitcoin: A Peer-to-Peer Electronic Cash System. *Decentralized business review*. SSRN: https://ssrn.com/abstract=3440802; http://dx.doi.org/10.2139/ssrn.3440802

Nam, K., Dutt, C. S., Chathoth, P., & Khan, M. S. (2021). Blockchain technology for smart city and smart tourism: Latest trends and challenges. *Asia Pacific Journal of Tourism Research*, *26*(4), 454–468. https://doi.org/10.1080/10941665.2019.1585376.

Nayal, K., Raut, R. D., Narkhede, B. E., Priyadarshinee, P., Panchal, G. B., & Gedam, V. V. (2021). Antecedents for blockchain technology-enabled sustainable agriculture supply chain. *Annals of Operations Research*. https://doi.org/10.1007/s10479-021-04423-3.

Niknejad, N., Ismail, W., Bahari, M., Hendradi, R., & Salleh, A. Z. (2021). Mapping the research trends on blockchain technology in food and agriculture industry: A bibliometric analysis. *Environmental Technology and Innovation*, *21*, 101272. https://doi.org/10.1016/j.eti.2020.101272.

Pakseresht, A., Yavari, A., Kaliji, S. A., & Hakelius, K. (2023). The intersection of blockchain technology and circular economy in the agri-food sector. *Sustainable Production and Consumption*, *35*, 260–274. https://doi.org/10.1016/j.spc.2022.11.002.

Pandey, V., Pant, M., & Snasel, V. (2022). Blockchain technology in food supply chains: Review and bibliometric analysis. *Technology in Society*, *69*(February), 101954. https://doi.org/10.1016/j.techsoc.2022.101954.

Panghal, A., Sindhu, S., Dahiya, S., Dahiya, B., & Mor, R. S. (2022). Benchmarking the Interactions among challenges for blockchain technology adoption : A circular economy perspective. *International Journal of Mathematical, Engineering and Management Sciences*, *7*(6), 859–872. https://doi.org/10.33889/IJMEMS.2022.7.6.054.

Peng, X., Zhang, X., Wang, X., Xu, J., Li, H., Zhao, Z., & Qi, Z. (2022). A refined supervision model of rice supply chain based on multi-blockchain. *Foods*, *11*(18), 1–25. https://doi.org/10.3390/foods11182785.

Pranto, T. H., Noman, A. A., Mahmud, A., & Haque, A. B. (2021). Blockchain and smart contract for IoT enabled smart agriculture. *PeerJ Computer Science*, *7*, 1–29. https://doi.org/10.7717/PEERJ-CS.407.

Sendros, A., Drosatos, G., Efraimidis, P. S., & Tsirliganis, N. C. (2022). Blockchain applications in agriculture: A scoping review. *Applied Sciences (Switzerland)*, 12(16). https://doi.org/10.3390/app12168061.

Sengupta, U., & Kim, H. M. (2021). Meeting changing customer requirements in food and agriculture through the application of blockchain technology. *Frontiers in Blockchain*, *4*(February), 1–10. https://doi.org/10.3389/fbloc.2021.613346.

Sharma, M., Khalil, A. A., & Daim, T. (2022). Blockchain technology adoption: Multinational analysis of the agriculture supply chain. *IEEE Transactions on Engineering Management*, 1–18. https://doi.org/10.1109/TEM.2022.3193688.

Singh, A. K., & Raza, Z. (2022). A framework for IoT and blockchain based smart food chain management system. *Concurrency and Computation: Practice and Experience*, (May), 1–28. https://doi.org/10.1002/cpe.7526.

Stranieri, S., Riccardi, F., Meuwissen, M. P. M., & Soregaroli, C. (2021). Exploring the impact of blockchain on the performance of agri-food supply chains. *Food Control*, *119*(May 2020), 107495. https://doi.org/10.1016/j.foodcont.2020.107495.

Talha Talukder, A. A., Mahmud, M. A. I., Sultana, A., Pranto, T. H., Haque, A. B., & Rahman, R. M. (2022). A customer satisfaction centric food delivery system based on blockchain and smart contract. *Journal of Information and Telecommunication*. https://doi.org/10.1080/24751839.2022.2117121.

Tan, A., Gligor, D., & Ngah, A. (2022). Applying blockchain for halal food traceability. *International Journal of Logistics Research and Applications*, *25*(6), 947–964. https://doi.org/10.1080/13675567.2020.1825653.

Tharatipyakul, A., & Pongnumkul, S. (2021). User interface of blockchain-based agri-food traceability applications: A review. *IEEE Access*, *9*, 82909–82929. https://doi.org/10.1109/ACCESS.2021.3085982.

Thomas, D. J., & Griffin, P. M. (1996). Coordinated supply chain management. *European Journal of Operational Research*, *94*(1), 1–15. https://doi.org/10.1016/0377-2217(96)00098-7.

Torky, M., & Hassanein, A. E. (2020). Integrating blockchain and the internet of things in precision agriculture: Analysis, opportunities, and challenges. *Computers and Electronics in Agriculture*, *178* (November 2019), 105476. https://doi.org/10.1016/j.compag.2020.105476.

Tripoli, M., & Schmidhuber, J. (2018). *Emerging Opportunities for the Application of Blockchain in the Agri-food Industry*. FAO and ICTSD: Rome and Geneva. Licence: CC BY-NC-SA 3.0 IGO

Trollman, H., Garcia-Garcia, G., Jagtap, S., & Trollman, F. (2022). Blockchain for eco-logically embedded coffee supply chains. *Logistics*, *6*(3), 43. https://doi.org/10.3390/logistics6030043.

van Hilten, M., Ongena, G., & Ravesteijn, P. (2020). Blockchain for organic food traceability: Case studies on drivers and challenges. *Frontiers in Blockchain*, *3*(September), 1–13. https://doi.org/10.3389/fbloc.2020.567175.

van Wassenaer, L., Verdouw, C., & Wolfert, S. (2021). What blockchain are we talking about? An analytical framework for understanding blockchain applications in agriculture and food. *Frontiers in Blockchain*, *4*(April), 1–8. https://doi.org/10.3389/fbloc.2021.653128.

Vu, N., Ghadge, A., & Bourlakis, M. (2022). Evidence-driven model for implementing blockchain in food supply chains. *International Journal of Logistics Research and Applications*, 1–21. https://doi.org/10.1080/13675567.2022.2115987.

Wang, L., He, Y., & Wu, Z. (2022). Design of a blockchain-enabled traceability system framework for food supply chains. *Foods, 11*(5), 1–18. https://doi.org/10.3390/foods11050744.

Xiong, H., Dalhaus, T., Wang, P., & Huang, J. (2020). Blockchain technology for agriculture: Applications and rationale. *Frontiers in Blockchain, 3*(February), 1–7. https://doi.org/10.3389/fbloc.2020.00007.

Zhang, L., & Kim, D. (2022). A peer-to-peer smart food delivery platform based on smart contract. *Electronics (Switzerland), 11*(12). https://doi.org/10.3390/electronics11121806.

Zhang, Y., Chen, L., Battino, M., Farag, M. A., Xiao, J., Simal-Gandara, J., Gao, H., & Jiang, W. (2022). Blockchain: An emerging novel technology to upgrade the current fresh fruit supply chain. *Trends in Food Science and Technology, 124*(July 2021), 1–12. https://doi.org/10.1016/j.tifs.2022.03.030.

Zheng, Z., Xie, S., Dai, H., Chen, X., & Wang, H. (2017). An overview of blockchain technology: Architecture, consensus, and future trends. *Proceedings - 2017 IEEE 6th International Congress on Big Data, BigData Congress 2017*, 557–564. https://doi.org/10.1109/BigDataCongress.2017.85.

Zhou, Q., Zhang, H., & Wang, S. (2022). Artificial intelligence, big data, and blockchain in food safety. *International Journal of Food Engineering, 18*(1), 1–14. https://doi.org/10.1515/ijfe-2021-0299.

Zkik, K., Belhadi, A., Rehman Khan, S. A., Kamble, S. S., Oudani, M., & Touriki, F. E. (2022). Exploration of barriers and enablers of blockchain adoption for sustainable performance: Implications for e-enabled agriculture supply chains. *International Journal of Logistics Research and Applications*, 1–38. https://doi.org/10.1080/13675567.2022.2088707.

4

BLOCKCHAIN TECHNOLOGY IN SHARING ECONOMY

Dorin-Cristian Coita and Olimpia Iuliana Ban

Understanding the Sharing Economy

The sharing economy is a business model that allows individuals to exchange resources, goods, or services through technology platforms. The sharing economy can include peer-to-peer (P2P) sharing of everything from cars and homes to tools and skills. Several reports demonstrate the increasing importance and evolution of the sharing economy as a significant economic and social trend in the 21st century (European Commission, 2016; PriceWaterhouseCoopers, 2014; Yaraghi & Ravi, 2017). According to the Global Sharing Economy Industry Research Report 2023 (*Absolute Reports®—Global Sharing Economy Industry Research Report 2023 Competitive Landscape Market*, 2023), the sharing economy market is expected to grow at a compound annual growth rate (CAGR) of 32% between 2023 and 2028. The key drivers of the sharing economy include the increasing adoption of mobile devices, the rise of the gig economy, and changing consumer preferences.

The key players in the global sharing economy market are Couchsurfing, Didi Global, BlaBlaCar, Lyft, Eatwith, Hubble, Fiverr, Uber, Lime, Steam, VaShare, Stashbee, JustPark, E-stronger, BHU Technology, Airbnb, Zipcar, Omni, Prosper, Snap, and Fon, and the sharing economy market from 2018 to 2028 is primarily split into shared transportation, shared space, shared financial services, shared food, shared health care, shared knowledge education, shared task service, shared items, and others. The report suggests that the sharing economy industry is poised for significant growth in the coming years, driven by technological innovation, changing consumer behavior, and increasing market penetration. Artificial intelligence and blockchain are among the prospects for the sharing economy industry and potential growth opportunities.

However, how could all this be possible? Several people can organize to pool their properties and provide access to them. Thus, the transition is made from

DOI: 10.4324/9781003351917-4

individual private property to access to the private property of several people. Entrepreneurs and market players have found ingenious ways (the platforms) to capitalize on available resources – privately owned by many people through shared access. Rachel Botsman, an expert on the sharing economy who co-authored the book *What's Mine Is Yours: How Collaborative Consumption Is Changing the Way We Live*, explains it as a system that allows individuals to share and access goods, services, and skills through online platforms (Botsman & Rogers, 2010). Botsman emphasizes that the sharing economy is distinguished by a culture of trust among strangers, facilitated by technology that enables people to connect, collaborate, and exchange resources. She underscores the social and economic benefits and sustainability of the sharing economy. Botsman ultimately envisions the sharing economy as a powerful transformative force which has the potential to revolutionize the way we consume, work, and live (Botsman & Rogers, 2010).

Arun Sundararajan, a professor of technology and management at New York University and the author of *The Sharing Economy: The End of Employment and the Rise of Crowd-Based Capitalism*, defines the sharing economy as an economic system that facilitates the sharing of underutilized resources by connecting individuals through digital platforms. According to Sundararajan, the sharing economy is a broad term encompassing different P2P exchange models, such as ride-sharing, home-sharing, and freelancing. He also emphasizes the importance of trust and reputation in the sharing economy, which enables individuals to transact with strangers without relying on traditional forms of regulation. Sundararajan views the sharing economy as a disruptive force that can create new economic opportunities, enhance consumer welfare, and promote sustainability (Sundararajan, 2017).

The fundamental concept behind the sharing economy is collaborative consumption, whereby individuals can pool resources to cut waste, enhance productivity, and reduce expenses (Botsman & Rogers, 2010; Gansky, 2010; Sundararajan, 2017). Essentially, the sharing economy depends on technology platforms to connect individuals who wish to share with those in need.

The Terms Used for the Sharing Economy

Other terms have been used for the sharing economy: "shared economy," "peer-to-peer economy," "collaborative consumption," "access economy," "platform-based economy," "community-based economy," "gift economy," "on-demand economy," or "collaborative economy." Ertz and Leblanc-Proulx (2018) consider the term "collaborative economy" to be more comprehensive than the oxymoron "sharing economy" or the narrower term "collaborative consumption."

Indeed, the term "sharing economy" seems to contradict itself since "sharing" typically refers to non-commercial, person-to-person interactions without monetary exchanges, while "economy" implies market transactions based on the self-interested exchange of money for goods or services. This has led to much debate about the term's appropriateness to describe the new wave of emerging businesses. Besides the terms mentioned above, other terms such as "the mesh economy," "peer-to-peer platforms," "the gig economy," or "concierge services" have been used. However, the most used term seems to be "sharing economy." Despite the overuse of the term "sharing," a name like "sharing economy" is still necessary to describe this phenomenon (Slee, 2015, p. 3).

Sharing Has Been a Long Tradition in Human History

Sharing goods and services within groups, families, and reference groups has been a longstanding tradition in human societies. Historically, people have exchanged resources such as food, clothing, and shelter to meet basic needs and foster social connections. Over time, sharing has evolved and taken on new forms, leading to the modern sharing economy concept (Botsman & Rogers, 2010; Schor, 2016). In the early 20th century, cooperatives emerged as a way for people to pool resources and share ownership of businesses and services. Cooperatives enabled individuals to share the benefits of ownership and participate in decision-making while reducing costs and increasing efficiency. In the post-World War II era, consumer culture and suburbanization increased individualism and private ownership of goods and services. However, sharing continued to exist within families and social networks. With the advent of the internet and digital technologies in the 21st century, the practice of sharing has transformed, leading to the emergence of the modern sharing economy. Online platforms and social networks have enabled individuals to share goods, services, and knowledge globally, leading to new forms of collaborative consumption and value creation. Sharing has become a central feature of today's digital age, enabling individuals to access goods and services more efficiently, reduce waste, and build social connections (Botsman & Rogers, 2010). Interest in this type of economics that strongly interferes with classical or commercial economics is evidenced by the number of research papers published on the subject.

Definitions and Characteristics of the Sharing Economy

Gerwe and Silva (2020) review a series of definitions of the "sharing economy" concept that reflect the differences in the understanding of the phenomenon in terms of delimiting the types of platforms that fall under this concept, the pro-profit or non-profit nature of this activity, and the types of resources that can be included in this activity (capital and/or human resources).

Cheng (2016), a leading name in the field, reviewed 66 articles on the sharing economy and ten papers related to tourism and hospitality published between 2010 and 2015. Ertz and Leblanc-Proulx (2018) presented a bibliometric analysis of 729 published articles to provide new insights into the evolution of the collaborative economy research field and its relationship to sustainable development. Prayag and Ozanne (2018) conducted a systematic literature review of 71 articles published between 2010 and 2016, focusing on P2P sharing economy accommodation. Sharing economy is not limited to P2P, understood as consumer-to-consumer (C2C), but can take on several forms, such as business-to-consumer (B2C) and business-to-business (B2B).

Cheng and Edwards (2019) reviewed the literature published on sharing economy with media discourse in tourism and hospitality from 2011 to 2016. Also, in 2019, Altinay and Taheri reviewed works in tourism and hospitality, tracking emerging themes such as disruptive behavior or trust as elements of the sharing economy.

Belarmino and Koh (2020) also focused their review of 107 articles on P2P accommodation services from 2010 to 2017. In 2022, Vila-Lopez and Küster-Boluda (2022) review the sharing-collaborative economy in the field of tourism in the post-COVID-19 pandemic era marching on several themes: trust, the need for innovation, authenticity, and control of the masses and sustainability in the sharing economy.

The definition of the concept follows the evolution of the application forms in practice. If initially it did not involve money and profit, the situation changed over time.

The key characteristics of the sharing economy can be seen in Table 4.1.

TABLE 4.1 Characteristics of the sharing economy extracted from the definitions

Characteristics	Definition	Other references
Both monetary and non-monetary transactions	"Transactions may be monetized or non-monetized and may take place for a variety of motivations ranging from very utilitarian 'You have what I want or need' commercial transactions to communitarian 'I give, swap or share because I want to help my community for a better world' exchanges" (Gyimóthy & Dredge, 2017, p. 16)	Botsman (2013) and Frenken and Schor (2019)
No transfer of ownership	"Transactions that may be market mediated in which no transfer of ownership takes place" (Bardhi & Eckhardt, 2012, p. 881)	Lessig (2008)
Temporary access Under-utilized physical assets, skills, or time	"An economic model based on sharing underutilized assets from spaces to skills to stuff for monetary or non-monetary benefits" (Botsman, 2013)	Frenken and Schor (2019)

(Continued)

TABLE 4.1 (Continued)

Characteristics	Definition	Other references
Facilitates P2P transactions, where both suppliers and consumers are natural persons Business-to-peer	"Such C2C transactions provide alternative travel goods (different from the commercial travel products) that can also enhance tourism sustainability by generating various forms of social value" (Sigala, 2015, p. 3)	Belarmino and Koh (2020), Cheng (2016), Frenken and Schor (2019), Prayag and Ozanne (2018) and Schor (2016)
Uses technology, one form being digital platforms that allow offline transactions between users	"(...) they are organized as digital platforms enabling offline transactions between users" (Gerwe and Silva, 2020, p. 8)	Belk (2014), Botsman (2013), Frenken and Schor (2019), and Sutherland and Jarrahi (2018)
To encourage emotions and experiences' memorability	"Furthermore, the meal-sharing platforms facilitated social interaction between tourists and hosts. Satisfactory interactions can occur as a result of this encounter. Therefore, service providers should offer comfortable and sincere atmospheres for guests" (Atsız et al., 2022, p. 18)	Mody et al. (2019) and Privitera and Abushena (2019)
The connection with sustainability	"It emphasizes the sharing of underutilized assets in ways that improve efficiency and sustainability" (Hossain, 2020, p. 1)	Curtis and Lehner (2019), Ertz and Leblanc-Proulx (2018), Heinrichs (2013) and Vila-Lopez and Küster-Boluda (2022)
Trust as a critical factor	"Users and potential users of the sharing economy need to place considerable trust in both the person and the platform with which they are dealing" (Ter Huurne et al., 2017, p. 1)	Altinay and Taheri (2019), Vila-Lopez and Küster-Boluda (2022) and Zhu et al. (2017)

Sharing Economy and the Tourism Industry

The sharing economy can significantly impact the tourism industry, and although much of the information about its effects on tourism originates from the platforms themselves, researchers, media outlets, tourism organizations, and international institutions have also begun to scrutinize these changes (European Commission, 2017). The sharing economy has transformed the tourism industry, presenting travelers with novel accommodations, activities, and transportation choices. In the sharing economy, anyone can become a tourism entrepreneur thanks to online platforms offering access to various services, some of which are of higher quality and more affordable than their conventional counterparts. As a result of this increased competition, established businesses are compelled to adapt by reducing their prices or enhancing their services.

The forms of sharing economy in tourism cover almost all package tour components, from accommodation to transportation to and within a destination, dining, and guided tours. According to Tussyadiah, the collaborative consumption trend significantly impacts the travel and tourism sector (Tussyadiah & Sigala, 2018). Peer-to-peer rental, swapping, and lending platforms are emerging, enabling locals to offer tourist services alongside traditional accommodation, transportation, and industry players. This disruption is changing the landscape of the travel and tourism industry.

One of the most significant impacts of the sharing economy on tourism is the rise of P2P accommodation (Sundararajan, 2017). Platforms like Airbnb, VRBO, Couchsurfing, and HomeAway have disrupted the traditional hotel industry and provided travelers with more affordable and unique lodging options (Gibbs et al., 2018; Guttentag, 2015). These platforms allow travelers to stay at the locals' homes or to book accommodation in private homes, apartments, or rooms, often cheaper than traditional hotels. This has increased the number of tourists who can travel and stay in more diverse locations, enhancing the overall tourism experience.

The sharing economy has also impacted transportation in tourism. Transportation service providers offer ride-sharing (when customers purchase a service and pay for a ride, rent or borrow a vehicle, or become members of a car-sharing scheme) or car-pooling (when people can give free rides in their vehicle or exchange a service) (Castellanos et al., 2022). Service providers like Uber, Lyft, Bolt, Grab, Careem, Go-Jek, Didi Chuxing, Ola, Via, Careem, Cabify, BlaBlaCar, Zipcar, Getaround, and Turo transformed how tourists get around, providing a more convenient and cost-effective alternative to traditional taxis and rental cars. This can make it more affordable and convenient for travelers to explore various destinations. Besides transportation, the platforms deliver car-pooling, event transportation, ride-hailing, taxi-hailing, food and goods delivery, freight services, payment services, bike-sharing, and electric vehicle rental services (Standing et al., 2019).

Another impact of the sharing economy on tourism is the rise of P2P tour and experience platforms such as Airbnb Experiences and Vayable. Locals offer travelers the opportunity to experience local activities and attractions with the guidance of a knowledgeable local host, providing them with a more authentic and personalized travel experience. Peer-to-peer dining platforms such as EatWith and Feastly allow travelers to experience local cuisine and culture by dining in the homes of local hosts. Digital nomads and remote workers increasingly use the sharing economy to find affordable and flexible accommodation and workspaces while they travel.

Benefits of the Sharing Economy for Tourism

The sharing economy has significantly impacted the tourism industry, offering a range of benefits for travelers and hosts, such as lower costs, greater flexibility, cultural immersion and authenticity, sustainability, and economic boost.

One of the most significant advantages of the sharing economy in tourism is the potential for lower costs. Sharing economy platforms like Airbnb and Couchsurfing offer affordable accommodation options compared to traditional hotels, making travel more accessible for budget-conscious travelers (Brauckmann, 2017; Kuhzady et al., 2022; Ozdemir & Turker, 2019). Sharing economy platforms provide greater flexibility for travelers, allowing them to customize their trips. They offer more comprehensive accommodation options, such as apartments, homes, and rooms, allowing travelers to choose a space that suits their needs and budget (Yu et al., 2022).

Sharing economy platforms also offer a more immersive travel experience. Travelers can stay with local hosts who can provide insider knowledge about the destination, recommend local attractions, and introduce travelers to local culture and customs (Paulauskaite et al., 2017). There are also social benefits to people's decisions to become hosts in P2P accommodation and rent out rooms in their properties. Many individuals participate in P2P hosting to alleviate loneliness (Farmaki & Stergiou, 2019). Sharing economy platforms promote sustainable travel practices by encouraging the use of existing resources rather than building new hotels or resorts. This can help reduce tourism's environmental impact and promote more forms of sustainability. Gössling and Hall identified 18 sustainability outcomes of sharing and collaborative economy that have been classified into four categories: (1) social (social effects, cultural learning, consumer empowerment, judgment culture); (2) economic (access, market concentration, competition, dependency structures, online reputation, business ethics, revenue distribution, value chains); (3) environmental (substitution, rebound effects); and (4) governance-related (big data, control, tax evasion, health, and safety) (Gössling & Michael Hall, 2019).

The sharing economy can also provide an economic boost to local communities, as it allows residents to monetize their spare space, skills, and time. It can create new opportunities for entrepreneurship, as people can start their businesses as hosts or service providers on sharing economy platforms. Economic benefits include the additional income for hosts, opportunities for micro-entrepreneurship (such as offering cleaning services and key handling), the generation of new jobs due to increased tourism, increased tax revenues, and the ability to cover temporarily spiking accommodation needs associated with significant events or natural disasters. P2P accommodation is a potential arena for micro-entrepreneurship, allowing hosts to make a living from renting their properties on a short-term basis and improving their living standards. Overall, P2P accommodation will enable individuals to gain additional income and enhance their quality of life by using idle assets (Farmaki & Miguel, 2022).

Entities of the Social Economy: For-Profit, Non-Profit, and Cooperatives

The conventional understanding of the sharing economy suggests that transactions primarily occur between individuals temporarily to access underutilized goods (Botsman & Rogers, 2010). However, not all platforms (and entities associated with them) operate in this manner. The sharing economy comprises enormous global companies like Uber or Airbnb and local grassroots initiatives. Moreover, there has been a progression from non-profit platforms such as Couchsurfing (established in 2004) to platforms that levy charges to cover expenses like BlaBlaCar, to businesses like Airbnb (founded in 2008) that generate substantial profits. Furthermore, Couchsurfing shifted in 2011 from a non-profit model to a profit-based model; more recently, there has been a rise in cooperatives and collectively owned and managed platforms (Gerwe & Silva, 2020). Cooperatives are considered the most important category of the social economy, alternatives to the profit-seeking business organizations of the capitalist economy (Coita et al., 2022). Cooperatives and the sharing economy have several common values and principles, such as cooperation, mutual benefit, and democratic decision-making (Fitzmaurice et al., 2020). The sharing economy phenomenon has led to the emergence of some cooperatively owned sharing economy platforms, such as Fairbnb, a cooperative alternative to Airbnb (Kirchner & Schüßler, 2020).

Criticism of the Sharing Economy

The sharing economy has numerous criticisms, conceptual uncertainty, legislative regulation, and application norms, reflecting concerns about its impact on workers, communities, and the broader economy, as well as concerns about its legal and regulatory status and the privacy and security of user data (Pedroni, 2019; Schor, 2016; Scholz, 2017; Slee, 2015). As it was born as a reaction to customer dissatisfaction with the traditional economy, initially, the sharing economy meant giving voluntarily and for free something that people have in excess to help, an act that may or may not imply reciprocity. The first forms of sharing economy (the notable example of Couchsurfing) were not monetized, and later cash payments were introduced not only to cover the costs but to obtain a (substantial) profit. The shift toward pro-profit activities from the sharing economy might represent a perversion of the original meaning (Lessig, 2008; Pedroni, 2019).

The sharing economy has been criticized for exploiting workers by classifying them as independent contractors rather than employees and for widening income inequality. This means they do not receive traditional employment benefits and protections, such as health insurance, paid time off, or worker's compensation. Critics argue that the sharing economy operates in a legal gray area, with many activities facilitated by sharing platforms not regulated by existing laws. Safety and liability issues may occur, as well as concerns about fair competition with established businesses subject to regulations. Likewise, the sharing economy could widen income inequality by creating a two-tier system where those who own and rent out assets benefit while those who do not are left behind (Schor, 2016). Additionally, low-income individuals may not have access to the resources necessary to participate in the sharing economy. The sharing economy has also been criticized for disrupting established industries, such as taxis, hotels, and restaurants, leading to job loss, economic instability in affected communities, and data privacy and security. Sharing platforms collect vast amounts of data on users, raising concerns about data privacy and security, particularly as these platforms have previously experienced data breaches (Scholz, 2017; Slee, 2015).

Another central idea of the sharing economy, "to rent out unused space" (Botsman, 2013), is currently redundant as long as individuals buy accommodation spaces specifically to be introduced on sharing economy platforms. "Airbnb hosts use their homes as sources of income to do things they otherwise would not be able to," says Fitzmaurice et al. (2020), which does not correspond to the current reality. Private individuals buy premises (e.g., apartments) that they rent advantageously (for them) to customers outside the traditional accommodation system. The fact that there are still people who make part of their housing available is true, but their share in total is debatable. If the spaces on the Airbnb platform do not represent the residence of the one who lists the space, the interaction with the owner is minimal, and the prices charged compete with those in the traditional system, doesn't the sharing economy tend to be an economy of entrepreneurs who want to avoid taxes and that is it?

However, apart from the issue of money, people sought human contact in the sharing economy, personalized exchange, and natural interaction/interest in solving a problem (Fitzmaurice et al., 2020). In this way, the sharing economy (even for profit) is the answer given to the standardized and impersonal services of companies. Customers prefer these services because the added value comes from the personification of the service; the problem solver has an identity to share with customers that give confidence. Thus, the goal of the sharing economy should be to create a more fair, sustainable, and socially connected society (Schor, 2016)

Other criticisms of the sharing economy are related to its lack of regulations, non-uniformity, and non-compliance with competition policies. Kirchner and Schüßler pointed out that a key element of the sharing economy is digital platforms; they have the role of mediating sharing activities between spatially dispersed buyers and sellers, often using mobile devices and application interfaces, all integrated into a digital marketplace. The problem is that "(…) sharing platforms operate in regulatory loopholes, treating the lack or lag of effective regulation and regulatory gray zones as a strategic opportunity," and this is one of the more severe problems that the sharing economy has (Kirchner & Schüßler, 2020, p. 3).

Blockchain and the Sharing Economy

Blockchain technology has distributed and decentralized characteristics that can improve business processes and operations through transparency, traceability, immutability, process automation, and disintermediation to innovate in the social economy and the tourism sectors. It provides the advantages of process automation and disintermediation, making the system more valuable to its principal participants.

A Problem Solver

The sharing economy was initially perceived to establish meaningful human relationships, but eventually, labor exploitation and massive valuations led to a new concept – the on-demand economy. Sharing was no longer integrated into the fabric of the economy, and alternative models such as platform cooperatives and equity crowdfunding were slow and legally complicated (Rustrum, 2018). Besides these, all traditional e-commerce models which rely on a centralized governance model for conducting business processes have several disadvantages, including C (Chang et al., 2022).

Even though the sharing economy has become a popular business model, the traditional governance model that relies on intermediaries to manage transactions and ensure trust between parties has been challenged by the rise of blockchain technology and smart contracts (Fiorentino & Bartolucci, 2021). The key characteristics of the sharing economy are the importance of reputation and trust (Hawlitschek et al., 2018), the need for flexible pricing models, and the decentralization of decision-making (Fiorentino & Bartolucci, 2021; Tumasjan & Beutel, 2019). Blockchain technology and smart contracts address these challenges by providing decentralized, transparent, and secure transaction platforms. The transparent and tamper-proof platforms for sharing economy transactions help establish trust between parties without intermediaries such as aggregators or marketplaces.

The More Collaborative and Community-Driven Sharing Economy

Another potential impact of blockchain on the sharing economy is the ability to create new decentralized marketplaces and platforms. For example, blockchain-based platforms can be designed to incentivize users to contribute to the platform and to reward them for their contributions. This can create a more collaborative and community-driven sharing economy that relies less on centralized intermediaries, contrary to so-called extractive companies like Airbnb and Uber. Assuming Uber and Airbnb were established as blockchain-based enterprises, they could provide an opportunity for long-term ownership value and reward individuals for their exceptional contributions as super hosts and frequent drivers. With blockchain technology, people might own a stake in an autonomous vehicle firm instead of possessing a car and could access a range of vehicles from anywhere across the globe (Rustrum, 2018). The use of blockchain technology will make it easier to shift the role of the crowd from simply providing capital and labor to becoming owners and operators of the marketplace in a decentralized manner (Sundararajan, 2017, p. 86).

Smart contracts can further enhance the efficiency and transparency of sharing economy transactions. Blockchain and smart contracts have great potential to transform the governance of the sharing economy to create decentralized networks that operate without a central authority. These platforms might use blockchain-based token systems to incentivize the participants to enable P2P transactions without the need for intermediaries and smart contracts to automate the payment process (Fiorentino & Bartolucci, 2021).

One of the main benefits of blockchain technology is that it provides a secure and transparent way to store and verify data (Huckle et al., 2016; Khan et al., 2020). This can be particularly useful in the sharing economy, where users often rely on intermediaries such as platforms, marketplaces, and payment processors to facilitate transactions and manage trust. With blockchain technology, users can transact directly without intermediaries, and the transactions can be securely and transparently recorded on the blockchain (Fiorentino & Bartolucci, 2021; Mehrwald et al., 2019). This can reduce transaction costs, increase trust and transparency, and facilitate the creation of new, decentralized sharing economy models. The storage facility concept is an ideal model for the sharing economy, allowing people to let go of underutilized assets and make money off items that otherwise remain unused. However, society may need to shift its views on ownership and material possessions to take full advantage of the sharing economy. Blockchain technology can facilitate a more secure and seamless sharing economy, which may redefine how we view consumerism and materialism.

Limits and Challenges

Despite the potential of the blockchain and other decentralized P2P technologies to handle a significant portion of the world's economic activity, several challenges must be addressed to realize their potential fully. Blockchain solves trust issues but transferring trust from blockchain to social economy systems is challenging and may require user-friendly interfaces (Hawlitschek et al., 2018). Security concerns continue, and scalability issues with the growing size of distributed ledgers across all clients continue to exist. Additionally, there are uncertainties about the scalability of blockchain-based applications. In payment systems like Bitcoin, which delay settlement, real-time payment processing, as handled by credit cards and mobile payment systems like PayPal, may require rebuilding the system (Sundararajan, 2017, p. 100).

One of the important challenges is the need for standardization and interoperability between different blockchain platforms. There are legal and regulatory challenges, such as ensuring compliance with existing regulations and establishing new legal frameworks for blockchain-based transactions (Fiorentino & Bartolucci, 2021). Nevertheless, blockchain technology can revolutionize the sharing economy by enabling the secure registration, documentation, and insurance of items for rent or lease and helping resolve insurance issues by allowing quick access to data about an item's condition, value, and provenance. Using blockchain and smart contract technologies can help develop a distributed governance model for achieving decentralized value creation and distribution in a new theory of value system with better support for social sharing and the sharing economy.

References

Absolute Reports®—Global Sharing Economy Industry Research Report 2023 Competitive Landscape Market. (2023). Retrieved April 25, 2023, from https://www.absolutereports.com/global-sharing-economy-industry-research-report-2023-competitive-landscape-market-22366527.

Altinay, L., & Taheri, B. (2019). Emerging themes and theories in the sharing economy: A critical note for hospitality and tourism. *International Journal of Contemporary Hospitality Management, 31*(1), 180–193.

Belarmino, A., & Koh, Y. (2020). A critical review of research regarding peer-to-peer accommodations. *International Journal of Hospitality Management, 84*, 102315.

Belk, R. (2014). You are what you can access: Sharing and collaborative consumption online. *Journal of Business Research, 67*(8), 1595–1600.

Botsman, R. (2013, November 21). *The Sharing Economy Lacks A Shared Definition.* Fast Company. https://www.fastcompany.com/3022028/the-sharing-economy-lacks-a-shared-definition.

Botsman, R., & Rogers, R. (2010). What's mine is yours. *The Rise of Collaborative Consumption, 1*. London: Collins.

Brauckmann, S. (2017). City tourism and the sharing economy–potential effects of online peer-to-peer marketplaces on urban property markets. *Journal of Tourism Futures, 3*(2), 114–126.

Castellanos, S., Grant-Muller, S., & Wright, K. (2022). Technology, transport, and the sharing economy: Towards a working taxonomy for shared mobility. *Transport Reviews, 42*(3), 318–336.

Chang, S. E., Chang, E. C., & Chen, Y. (2022). Blockchain meets sharing economy: A case of smart contract enabled ridesharing service. *Sustainability, 14*(21), 13732.

Cheng, M. (2016). Sharing economy: A review and agenda for future research. *International Journal of Hospitality Management, 57*, 60–70.

Cheng, M., & Edwards, D. (2019). A comparative automated content analysis approach on the review of the sharing economy discourse in tourism and hospitality. *Current Issues in Tourism, 22*(1), 35–49.

Coita, D. C., Fotea, S., Prisac, I., & Nemteanu, M. S. (2022). *Managementul și marketingul organizațiilor nonprofit.* Editura Economică.

Curtis, S. K., & Lehner, M. (2019). Defining the sharing economy for sustainability. *Sustainability, 11*(3), 567.

Ertz, M., & Leblanc-Proulx, S. (2018). Sustainability in the collaborative economy: A bibliometric analysis reveals emerging interest. *Journal of Cleaner Production, 196*, 1073–1085.

European Commission. (2016). *A European Agenda for the Collaborative Economy.*

European Commission. (2017). *Tourism and the Sharing Economy.* https://www.europarl.europa.eu/RegData/etudes/BRIE/2017/595897/EPRS_BRI(2017)595897_EN.pdf.

Farmaki, A., & Miguel, C. (2022). Peer-to-peer accommodation in Europe: Trends, challenges and opportunities. In Česnuitytė, V., Klimczuk, A., Miguel, C., & Avram, G. (eds.), *The Sharing Economy in Europe: Developments, Practices, and Contradictions* (pp. 115–136).

Farmaki, A., & Stergiou, D. P. (2019). Escaping loneliness through Airbnb host-guest interactions. *Tourism Management, 74,* 331–333.

Fiorentino, S., & Bartolucci, S. (2021). Blockchain-based smart contracts as new governance tools for the sharing economy. *Cities, 117,* 103325.

Fitzmaurice, C. J., Ladegaard, I., Attwood-Charles, W., Cansoy, M., Carfagna, L. B., Schor, J. B., & Wengronowitz, R. (2020). Domesticating the market: Moral exchange and the sharing economy. *Socio-Economic Review, 18*(1), 81–102.

Frenken, K., & Schor, J. (2019). Putting the sharing economy into perspective. In *A Research Agenda for Sustainable Consumption Governance* (pp. 121–135). Edward Elgar Publishing.

Gansky, L. (2010). *The Mesh: Why the Future of Business Is Sharing.* Penguin.

Gerwe, O., & Silva, R. (2020). Clarifying the sharing economy: Conceptualization, typology, antecedents, and effects. *Academy of Management Perspectives, 34*(1), 65–96.

Gibbs, C., Guttentag, D., Gretzel, U., Morton, J., & Goodwill, A. (2018). Pricing in the sharing economy: A hedonic pricing model applied to Airbnb listings. *Journal of Travel & Tourism Marketing, 35*(1), 46–56.

Gössling, S., & Michael Hall, C. (2019). Sharing versus collaborative economy: How to align ICT developments and the SDGs in tourism? *Journal of Sustainable Tourism, 27*(1), 74–96.

Guttentag, D. (2015). Airbnb: Disruptive innovation and the rise of an informal tourism accommodation sector. *Current Issues in Tourism, 18*(12), 1192–1217.

Hawlitschek, F., Notheisen, B., & Teubner, T. (2018). The limits of trust-free systems: A literature review on blockchain technology and trust in the sharing economy. *Electronic Commerce Research and Applications, 29,* 50–63. https://doi.org/10.1016/j.elerap.2018.03.005.

Huckle, S., Bhattacharya, R., White, M., & Beloff, N. (2016). Internet of things, blockchain and shared economy applications. *Procedia Computer Science, 98,* 461–466.

Khan, U., An, Z. Y., & Imran, A. (2020). A blockchain ethereum technology-enabled digital content: Development of trading and sharing economy data. *IEEE Access, 8,* 217045–217056.

Kirchner, S., & Schüßler, E. (2020). Regulating the sharing economy: A field perspective. In Maurer, I., Mair, J., and Oberg, A. (eds.), *Theorizing the Sharing Economy: Variety and Trajectories of New Forms of Organizing.* Vo. 66, 215–236. Bingley: Emerald Publishing Limited. https://doi.org/10.1108/S0733-558X20200000066010

Kuhzady, S., Seyfi, S., & Béal, L. (2022). Peer-to-peer (P2P) accommodation in the sharing economy: A review. *Current Issues in Tourism, 25*(19), 3115–3130.

Lessig, L. (2008). *Remix: Making Art and Commerce Thrive in the Hybrid Economy.* Bloomsbury Academic.

Mehrwald, P., Treffers, T., Titze, M., & Welpe, I. M. (2019). Application of blockchain technology in the sharing economy: A model of trust and intermediation. *Proceedings of the 52nd Hawaii International Conference on System Sciences,* 4585–4594.

Mody, M., Suess, C., & Lehto, X. (2019). Going back to its roots: Can hospitableness provide hotels competitive advantage over the sharing economy? *International Journal of Hospitality Management, 76,* 286–298.

Ozdemir, G., & Turker, D. (2019). Institutionalization of the sharing in the context of Airbnb: A systematic literature review and content analysis. *Anatolia, 30*(4), 601–613.

Paulauskaite, D., Powell, R., Coca-Stefaniak, J. A., & Morrison, A. M. (2017). Living like a local: Authentic tourism experiences and the sharing economy. *International Journal of Tourism Research, 19*(6), 619–628.

Pedroni, M. (2019). Sharing economy as an anti-concept. *First Monday*.

Prayag, G., & Ozanne, L. K. (2018). A systematic review of peer-to-peer (P2P) accommodation sharing research from 2010 to 2016: Progress and prospects from the multi-level perspective. *Journal of Hospitality Marketing & Management, 27*(6), 649–678.

PriceWaterhouseCoopers. (2014). *The Sharing Economy: How Will It Disrupt Your Business?* https://pwc.blogs.com/files/sharing-economy-final_0814.pdf.

Privitera, D., & Abushena, R. (2019). The home as a consumption space: Promoting social eating. In Byrom, J., Medway, D., Cavicchi, A., & Santini, C. (eds.), *Case Studies in Food Retailing and Distribution* (pp. 69–86). Elsevier.

Rustrum, C. (2018, August 14). The future of blockchain—Bridging the sharing economy—A TEDx talk. *HackerNoon.Com.* https://medium.com/hackernoon/the-future-of-blockchain-bridging-the-sharing-economy-a-tedx-talk-b46b897d27f8.

Scholz, T. (2017). *Uberworked and Underpaid: How Workers Are Disrupting the Digital Economy*. John Wiley & Sons.

Schor, J. (2016). Debating the sharing economy. *Journal of Self-Governance and Management Economics, 4*(3), 7–22.

Slee, T. (2015). *What's Yours Is Mine*. OR Books.

Standing, C., Standing, S., & Biermann, S. (2019). The implications of the sharing economy for transport. *Transport Reviews, 39*(2), 226–242.

Sundararajan, A. (2017). *The Sharing Economy: The End of Employment and the Rise of Crowd-Based Capitalism*. MIT press.

Sutherland, W., & Jarrahi, M. H. (2018). The sharing economy and digital platforms: A review and research agenda. *International Journal of Information Management, 43*, 328–341.

Tumasjan, A., & Beutel, T. (2019). Blockchain-based decentralized business models in the sharing economy: A technology adoption perspective. *Business Transformation through Blockchain: Volume I* (pp. 77–120).

Tussyadiah, I. P., & Sigala, M. (2018). Shareable tourism: Tourism marketing in the sharing economy. *Journal of Travel & Tourism Marketing, 35*(1), 1–4.

Vila-Lopez, N., & Küster-Boluda, I. (2022). Sharing-collaborative economy in tourism: A bibliometric analysis and perspectives for the post-pandemic era. *Tourism Economics, 28*(1), 272–288.

Yaraghi, N., & Ravi, S. (2017). The current and future state of the sharing economy. *SSRN Electronic Journal*. https://doi.org/10.2139/ssrn.3041207.

Yu, M., Cheng, M., Yu, Z., Tan, J., & Li, Z. (2022). Investigating Airbnb listings' amenities relative to hotels. *Current Issues in Tourism, 25*(19), 3168–3185.

Zhu, G., So, K. K. F., & Hudson, S. (2017). Inside the sharing economy: Understanding consumer motivations behind the adoption of mobile applications. *International Journal of Contemporary Hospitality Management, 29*(9), 2218–2239.

5

TRANSFORMING TOURISM AND HOSPITALITY

The Innovative Potential of Non-Fungible Tokens (NFTs)

Irem Onder and Horst Treiblmaier

Introduction

Blockchain technology has been one of the most transformative and disruptive innovations of the 21st century. At its core, blockchain is a decentralized, digital ledger that records transactions in a secure and transparent manner. Originally developed as the underlying technology for cryptocurrencies such as Bitcoin, blockchain has since been applied to a wide range of industries, from finance to healthcare. According to Iansiti and Lakhani (2017), blockchain technology serves as a fundamental building block for developing new economic and social systems. Although it is commonly associated with cryptocurrencies like Bitcoin and Ether, recent advancements have showcased the technology's vast potential. Smart contracts, combined with tokenization, have the ability to create new revenue streams for the hospitality and tourism industry. This concept is often referred to as the "Internet of Value," which entails the digitalization of assets such as intellectual and digital properties, equity, and wealth, and their secure and automated transfer (Goanta, 2020, p. 142). Since blockchain technology is a disruptive force, organizations need to strategically approach and integrate it to ensure competitiveness in the long term (Rejeb et al., 2020).

Previous research indicates the potential benefits of blockchain use in tourism and hospitality (Önder & Gunter, 2022; Önder & Treiblmaier, 2018; Ozdemir et al., 2020), and further research is strongly recommended to better understand the impact of blockchain and cryptocurrencies on international travel (Assaf et al., 2022). According to Rashideh (2020), the accommodation sector is primed to implement blockchain solutions for financial management, inventory control, and recording guest histories. In this regard, travel agencies such as Webjet in Australia,

DOI: 10.4324/9781003351917-5

Accenture in Canada, TravelChain in Russia, and Cool Cousin in London have already begun to implement blockchain. Given the complexity of the technology and the uncertainty regarding viable use cases, the industry and researchers need to work together to find promising tourism applications of this technology that yield new products and services (Önder & Gunter, 2022).

One of the most exciting and rapidly growing applications of blockchain technology is in the form of non-fungible tokens (NFTs). NFTs are unique digital tokens that represent ownership of a specific asset or piece of content. They have quickly gained traction in the world of art, music, and sports, where they allow creators to sell their work as one-of-a-kind items. NFTs are different from traditional cryptocurrencies in that they are not interchangeable, meaning that each token is unique and represents a specific asset. NFTs are quickly gaining traction in the world of digital assets, and their potential applications are numerous. One industry that stands to benefit from NFTs is tourism and hospitality, where these tokens have the potential to transform the way people experience and engage with the sector. For example, a hotel could create an NFT that represents a stay in their presidential suite, complete with special amenities and personalized services. This NFT could be sold to a collector or enthusiast who wants to own a piece of the hotel's history, or it could be used as a way to incentivize loyalty program members to earn points toward a stay in the suite. In addition, NFTs could be used to represent access to exclusive locations or events, such as a private tour of a famous landmark or a VIP ticket to a music festival. These tokens could be sold to collectors or travelers who want to experience something unique and memorable, and they could also be used as a way for destinations to promote themselves and attract new visitors.

The tourism and hospitality industry has also started exploring the potential applications of NFTs. By creating and selling NFTs, businesses in this sector can provide guests with unique and exclusive experiences that are not available through traditional means. These tokens can represent access to exclusive locations or events, personalized services and amenities, or even ownership of a part of a hotel's history. Some examples of NFTs in this sector include Marriot Bonvoy, which is an NFT collection and was debut on December 4, 2021 through Miami Beach Art Basel (Adele, 2021); Taco Bell also issued taco-themed NFTs on an NFT platform, Rareable, and was sold out in under 30 minutes (Clark, 2021); McDonald's created NFTs to represent McRib for its 40th anniversary (Rosenblatt, 2021).

The use of blockchain and NFTs in the tourism and hospitality industry has the potential to revolutionize the way guests experience and engage with this sector. By leveraging the transparency and security of blockchain technology, businesses can create new revenue streams, incentivize loyalty, and promote destinations. In this chapter, we will explore the potential benefits and challenges of using blockchain and NFTs in the tourism and hospitality industry and examine some of the innovative use cases that have emerged in this field.

Blockchain and Tokens

Defining Tokens and NFTs

A token may be characterized as a value unit that signifies an asset, a particular use, or a method of payment, as described by Treiblmaier (2021, p. 2). Asset tokenization is the act of creating a digital blockchain token that embodies a real-world, exchangeable asset (Laurent et al., 2018, p. 63). As a result, both tangible and intangible assets can be tokenized, and any item with unique identifying attributes can be transformed into a NFT. Various token standards, such as ERC-20, ERC-721, and ERC-1155 on the Ethereum blockchain, are available on multiple platforms to identify a token's specific characteristics.

Treiblmaier (2021) classifies tokens into three categories: payment, utility, and investment. Payment tokens are primarily employed for making transactions, whereas utility tokens bestow rights upon their owners, and investment tokens (also known as security tokens) are purchased to acquire a stake in an asset or establish a loan.

Regarding tradability, tokens can be classified as either fungible or non-fungible. Fungible tokens have identical forms and values, similar to banknotes. NFT, however, represent unique assets. It is essential to note, however, that blockchain's traceability feature can sometimes blur the distinction between fungible and NFTs. For instance, a specific Bitcoin might be considered a fungible token, but its transaction history can be traced, enabling users to reject coins that have been involved in illicit activities. Table 5.1 depicts the distinctions between fungible tokens and NFTs.

NFTs have a number of unique properties that make them appealing to both buyers and sellers. First, NFTs are non-fungible, which means that they are unique and cannot be replaced. This makes them ideal for representing items that are

TABLE 5.1 Fungible and NFT differences

Feature	Fungible tokens	NFTs
Value	Identical in value	Unique and distinct value
Interchangeability	Interchangeable with one another	Not interchangeable
Use cases	Currency, payment tokens	Collectibles, digital art, gaming
Token standards (Ethereum)	ERC-20	ERC-721, ERC-1155
Rarity	Common, can be easily replicated	Rare, hard to replicate
Example	Bitcoin, Ether, Stablecoins	CryptoKitties, digital art
Uniqueness	No unique attributes	Unique attributes and metadata
Traceability	Tracked collectively	Tracked individually

also unique, such as works of art or collectibles. Second, NFTs are verifiable. The ownership of an NFT is stored on a blockchain, which is a secure and transparent ledger. This means that buyers can be confident that they are buying the real thing. Third, NFTs are transferable. They can be bought, sold, or traded on decentralized exchanges. This makes them a liquid asset that can be easily exchanged for other cryptocurrencies or fiat currencies.

NFTs are still in their early stages of development, but they have the potential to revolutionize the way we interact with digital assets. By making it possible to own and trade unique digital items, NFTs could open up new markets for artists, creators, and collectors. They could also play a role in the development of new applications, such as decentralized gaming and virtual reality.

Here are some examples of how NFTs are being used today:

Art: NFTs are being used to sell digital art, including paintings, photographs, and music. For example, the artist Beeple sold a collection of NFTs for $69.3 million at a Christie's auction in 2021.

Gaming: NFTs are being used to create unique in-game items, such as weapons, skins, and pets. These items can be bought, sold, or traded by players, which adds a new layer of value to the game.

Collectibles: NFTs are being used to create unique collectibles, such as trading cards, sports memorabilia, and even concert tickets. These items can be bought, sold, or traded by collectors, which adds a new level of scarcity and value.

NFT Example

Figure 5.1 shows an example of NFT art sold on the Mintable platform. On this page, all the corresponding information of the NFT is published, including the NFT name (i.e., Abstract Geometric Shape), artist name (i.e., Artist), seller name (i.e., Artist) and rating (from 1 to 5), and NFT description and keywords for finding similar NFTs (i.e., geometric, abstract, shape). In addition, the price of the NFT is shown both in US dollars ($200.57) and Ether (0.1111ETH). The purchase of an NFT can be done with cryptocurrency or credit card, giving buyers flexibility and the creators of NFTs an opportunity to expand the number of potential buyers by including those who cannot or do not want to use cryptocurrencies.

The pricing reflects the rules of the smart contract for this type of NFT. Said rules include copyright (whether the copyright of the NFT is transferred or not), download access (whether the NFT is downloadable or not), and reselling rules (whether the buyer can resell the NFT or not). For example, if an individual purchases the NFT shown in Figure 5.1, the copyright of the NFT is not transferred, but the NFT is downloadable and resellable based on the smart contract. Furthermore, because the artist (the seller in this case) keeps the copyright but the NFT is resellable, meaning that if the buyer sells this NFT to someone else, then the artist will get a copyright fee as identified in the smart contract.

To make a purchase using cryptocurrency, the first step is to create a crypto wallet and acquire some cryptocurrency. The next step is to set up an account in an

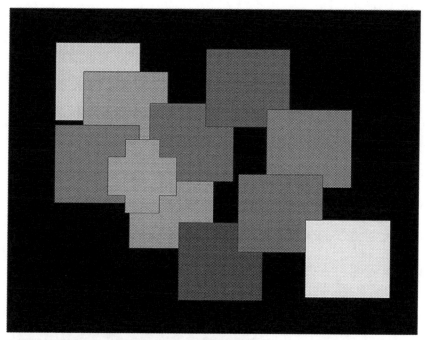

Abstract Geometric Shape	
Original artwork by Artist	Token ID: 00000000
Seller: Artist	Price: $200.57 or (0.1111ETH)
Store: Mintable	Keywords: Geometric, abstract, shape
Item description: Abstract geometric shapes created by Artist	Copyright Transferred: No Downloadable file: Yes Resellabe: Yes

FIGURE 5.1   NFT example on the Mintable platform.

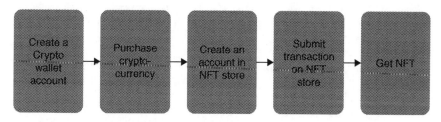

FIGURE 5.2   Steps for purchasing NFTs (adapted from Mintable.com).

NFT marketplace such as Mintable, OpenSea, SuperRare, or Nifty Gateway. Most NFT marketplaces sell via online auctions, meaning that the buyer needs to make a bid for the NFT. Once the transaction is submitted to the NFT marketplace, the buyer receives the NFT (see Figure 5.2).

How to Create (Mint) and Sell NFTs

To make NFTs, the creator needs to use a minting platform such as Mintable, Mintbase, Rarible, or Cargo. Any content the NFT creator owns, such as files, artwork, PDF, research, and images, can be turned into NFTs. This process is known as minting an NFT. NFTs are smart contract-based digital items on the blockchain. Users can create their own NFTs as well as buy and sell them on the blockchain. The sales are often auction-based, and upon payment, the NFT is deposited into the digital wallet of the buyer, thus authenticating the buyer as the new official owner of the NFT in question. In this manner, artists can create NFTs of their works and musicians can sell limited-edition album covers as NFTs.

Before creating an NFT, a seller needs to select a store to sell it on. Sellers who do not wish to create a store themselves can use Mintable or other minting platforms, in which case the minting company gets a percentage of every marketplace sale. The seller can create an NFT by filling out the details of the item, such as the title, tags, price, copyright, whether it is resellable or not, image view and description, name of the item, and the category to which it belongs (e.g., artwork, music file, media file). After the information is complete, the asset becomes an

TABLE 5.2 Advantages and disadvantages of NFTs

Advantages	Disadvantages
Digital ownership and provenance: NFTs allow for verification of ownership and provenance of digital assets, enabling creators to assert ownership and buyers to confirm authenticity.	*Environmental impact:* The energy-intensive nature of the blockchain networks to mint (create) and trade NFTs raises environmental concerns.
Royalties for creators: NFTs enable creators to receive royalties from secondary sales, providing them with a continuous revenue stream.	*Market volatility:* The NFT market is highly volatile, and prices can fluctuate dramatically, which can lead to potential losses for creators and buyers.
Programmability: Using smart contracts, NFTs can be programmed with various features such as time-based access, unlocking additional content, or integrating with other digital assets.	*Interoperability issues*: NFTs are often tied to specific platforms or blockchain, leading to a lack of interoperability between different ecosystems.
Digital asset protection: NFTs offer improved protection for digital assets, preventing unauthorized copying and distribution.	*High transaction fees:* The process of minting, buying, and selling NFTs can incur high transaction fees on certain blockchain networks.
Access to new revenue streams: NFTs enable creators to monetize digital assets that were previously difficult to sell or license, opening up new revenue streams.	*Legal and regulatory uncertainty*: The legal framework surrounding NFTs and digital asset ownership is still evolving, leading to potential challenges and uncertainties for creators and buyers.

NFT on a blockchain and the seller can post it on a marketplace. The buyer needs to have a digital wallet to purchase NFTs. For instance, when using the Mintable marketplace, the buyer needs to have an Ethereum wallet. The digital currency and the NFTs will be kept in the buyer's digital wallet. For trading NFTs, the digital wallet (e.g., MetaMask, Trust Wallet, and Rainbow) must be connected to decentralized applications (dApps) (Burks, 2021).

We can summarize the general advantages and disadvantages of NFTs as shown in Table 5.2.

Benefits of NFTs for the Tourism Industry and Its Consumers

One advantage of tokenizing real-world assets is that these tokens are easily tradable on blockchains via secondary markets (Laurent et al., 2018). By tokenizing and selling an asset, the creator or owner receives a financial gain. The benefits for a tourism destination that owns a tokenized asset include receiving extra financial contributions from consumers on virtual world blockchains. A destination can also receive additional advertising income because it exists as an NFT on the blockchain. In addition, new work opportunities open up for artists and computer programmers who create digital assets as NFTs. NFTs can be sold to collectors or enthusiasts, generating additional revenue streams for tourism and hospitality businesses. They can also be used as a way to incentivize loyalty program members to earn points toward specific experiences or services, leading to increased spending and repeat visits.

One benefit of buying NFTs for the consumer is that they can be resold again at higher values. Because NFTs are scarce, their value is expected to increase over time in case they represent an appealing asset, making them a novel investment opportunity. The value of an NFT is usually determined as would be the case on an art auction circuit. Further benefits of NFTs for consumers can be designed and implemented by the creators of those NFTs. For instance, NFTs can be used to offer exclusive and unique experiences, such as access to private tours, VIP tickets, or personalized services, that cannot be replicated elsewhere. This creates a sense of exclusivity and value for guests, which can lead to increased customer loyalty and positive word-of-mouth recommendations.

NFTs can be used as a creative marketing tool to promote destinations, hotels, and events. By showcasing unique experiences or events that can only be accessed through NFTs, tourism and hospitality businesses can attract new visitors and differentiate themselves from competitors. Tokenized assets can create a market specifically for tourism products, including virtual tours in tokenized museums or other heritage sites. A destination can create a portfolio of tourism products such as a three-day tour of Istanbul, a visit to the Louvre, and the ability to shop for local products. For instance, Amazon already launched tourism experience products on its Amazon Explore page during the COVID-19 pandemic. Users can purchase live and interactive tours with local guides, as well as shop in local stores by paying through the Amazon website. The products are not only city tours but also culinary experiences. For instance, an individual can purchase a sushi-making class with a chef from Japan. This is a live and interactive experience as well. Technology-driven tourism experiences similar to tokenized destinations and built heritage assets result in the co-creation of experiences.

Moreover, NFTs can provide a secure way to protect and authenticate valuable assets, such as artwork or historic artifacts, that are owned by tourism and hospitality businesses. This can prevent fraud and counterfeiting, ensuring the authenticity and value of these assets.

The COVID-19 pandemic has changed the way we live and work. In the past two years, we have become increasingly reliant on technology for our health, safety, and entertainment. This has led to a growing interest in tokenized assets, which can provide a new way to experience the world without leaving our homes.

One example of how tokenized assets can be used to enhance tourism is through the creation of digital twins. A digital twin is a virtual replica of a real-world object or location. It can be used to provide visitors with a 360-degree view of a destination, as well as access to information and experiences that would not be possible in the physical world. For example, a digital twin of the Eiffel Tower could allow visitors to learn about its history, architecture, and engineering. It could also provide them with virtual tours of the tower's interior, as well as access to exclusive content, such as behind-the-scenes footage and interviews with the tower's designers and engineers.

Tokenized assets can also be used to create new forms of entertainment. For example, a company could create a token that allows holders to access exclusive content, such as early access to new movies or video games. They could also use tokens to create virtual worlds, where users can interact with each other and explore new environments. This can also strengthen the brand image. Creating and selling NFTs can help businesses in the tourism and hospitality industry to strengthen their brand image by showcasing their innovative and forward-thinking approach to hospitality. In return, NFTs can appeal to tech-savvy travelers and position tourism and hospitality businesses as forward-thinking and innovative.

The COVID-19 pandemic has shown us how vulnerable we are. It has also shown us the importance of having access to entertainment and education, even when we cannot leave our homes. Tokenized assets can provide a new way to experience the world without leaving our homes, and they can help us to stay connected with each other, even when we are physically apart.

Theoretical Perspectives

Previous academic research has illustrated how theory can help to explore, explain, and predict phenomena in tourism. Furthermore, it has helped to create an incremental research agenda in which new findings can be easily combined with previous ones. In this respect, tokenization can be seen as a part of an ongoing digital transformation that completely restructures organizations, the relations with their general environments, and how they interact with their customers (Soulard et al., 2019). Hence, we present the following three theories that are well-suited to investigate the respective areas.

The Internal Perspective: Resource-Based View of the Firm

The resource-based view of a company focuses on the resources that a company possesses as a source of competitive advantage (Wernerfelt, 1984). Tourism and hospitality research has previously applied this theoretical lens to identify those decisive factors that help organizations remain competitive (Camisón et al., 2016; Duarte Alonso et al., 2021). When it comes to tokenization, the question arises of whether the process as such will help companies to reap additional value. This may indeed be the case for some organizations which might benefit from the first mover effect, but over time, it stands to reason that this effect might wear off and more and more organizations will learn which assets they can tokenize and how to best market them. However, a thorough investigation is needed on how the respective features of tokenized assets, such as the aforementioned possibility to gain ongoing profits due to smart contracts, can be best exploited by the various organizations on what kind of impact that might have on (dis)intermediation, organizational boundaries, business models, and, ultimately, their relationships with customers.

The External Perspective: Dynamic Capabilities

Dynamic capabilities were defined by Teece et al. (1997, 516) as "the firm's ability to integrate, build, and reconfigure internal and external competencies to address rapidly-changing environments." This perspective extends the internal focus of the resource-based view and considers the external business environment which might necessitate a constant adjustment of the resource mix to achieve a sustained competitive advantage. In tourism research, dynamic capabilities have been used to investigate the need for travel agencies to restructure their business (Abrate et al., 2020) and to gain an understanding of how tourism organizations can best respond to natural disasters (Jiang et al., 2022). When it comes to tokenization, companies' external environment is complex and ever-changing. It pertains not only to the technological underpinning of blockchain technology but also to the legal regulations in this volatile space. Academic research is, therefore, needed to describe and delimit the various environments and gain a better understanding of how the reciprocal relationship between a tourism organization and its external surroundings might offer new opportunities and threats.

The Consumer Perspective: Technology Adoption and Acceptance

The adoption and acceptance of technology constitute a broad and well-established field of academic research that has yielded numerous publications over the years. Many publications in this field draw on seminal research that originates in the area of diffusion of innovation and has yielded numerous refined models such as the technology acceptance model (TAM) and the unified theory of acceptance and use of technology (UTAUT) (Rogers, 2003; Venkatesh et al., 2003). In this regard, tourism research is no exception and has applied these models to a wide range of problems, such as managers' decisions to adopt marketing decision support systems (Wöber & Gretzel, 2000) or, more recently, the adoption of AI-based chatbots (Pillai & Sivathanu, 2020). Given that these models are fairly generic, an adaptation is needed to tailor them for tokenization applications. Further research might also want to delve deeper and investigate, for example, what factors determine the ease of use of a specific application or, in a design science paradigm, how solutions can be created that minimize users' cognitive efforts to apply these applications. Additionally, the relative importance of the diverse components of these models, such as social influence or hedonic motivations, needs to be clarified for token applications. Figure 5.3 summarizes the aforementioned theories and illustrates the particular views.

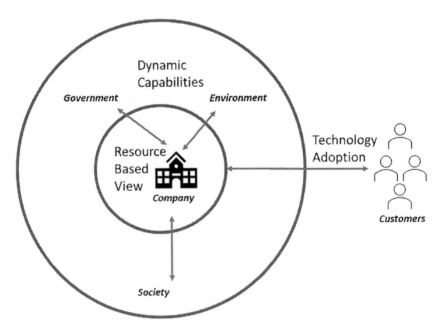

FIGURE 5.3   Three theoretical perspectives on tokenization in the tourism industry.

Conclusion and Discussion

As we are shifting toward a decentralized economy, new opportunities are arising. One of these opportunities is found in tokenization based on public blockchains. The nature of tourism and hospitality assets and their product offerings makes them suitable for numerous tokenization opportunities, thus creating alternative ways of generating revenues. This offers substantial implications for academics and practitioners.

Implications for Academics

The tokenization options outlined in this conceptual chapter pose the next step in the further digitalization and transformation of the tourism and hospitality industry. While blockchain applications have already been developed to facilitate booking, payment, and supply chain processes within the industry, the tokenization of physical and virtual assets is a comparatively new and unexplored topic. In this regard, a substantial amount of rigorous research is needed to better understand how this phenomenon can potentially contribute value, how it will shape the industry, and which factors might decide its ultimate adoption. We have suggested three theoretical perspectives as potential starting points. Of course, this does not exclude other theoretical approaches, but the investigation of how tokens can provide value for tourism organizations by strengthening their internal resources, shaping their external relationships, and being accepted by customers will provide a solid starting point for scholars working in that area. While a solid amount of literature on the respective theories already exists, further operationalizations and modifications are needed to account for the idiosyncrasies of tokenization. This is especially important in an area that is characterized by a plethora of different applications, each with its unique properties and features. By carefully investigating and structuring the domain, academia will be able to lay the foundation for future incremental research and create an understanding of how tokenization will impact the industry and its customers alike.

Implications for Practitioners

Tourism and hospitality assets consist of a wide array of cultural and heritage attractions, including cities as destinations, historical artifacts housed in museums, and the like. It is possible to represent specific resources and assets of the industry by some predetermined or assessed numbers of tokens on a public blockchain, with each token standing for a fractional value of a given attraction or artifact with its own NFT. Thus, issued blockchain-based tokens can be easily created, traded, stored, and transferred in the digital world. Through fractional ownership, tourism assets of all sizes can be made accessible on a secure online platform. They also become tradeable on secondary markets, thus allowing a broader base of investors to participate in the financial ecosystem toward the generation of new revenues. Moreover, the destination or the attraction would directly benefit from the financial gain without the need of a middleman such as a bank. Tokenized assets remove both physical barriers and infrastructural limits.

In addition to creating financial viability, the tokenization of tourism attractions via NFTs offers several advantages for sustainable tourism practices and managing attractions more efficiently. By holding tokens, travelers are no longer mere consumers but also, to some extent, owners of the asset, thus fostering a sense of shared responsibility for the product and its consumption and preservation. Sustainably managing such a product shows that both demand and supply are in the best interest of the token holder as well as the attraction manager. Through the tokenization process of the product or assets, DMOs and destination managers are better positioned to sustain and increase their revenue options. Increased revenues would also allow them to manage their assets more effectively. It is well known that most visits to certain destinations and attractions are seasonal. This reality makes the amount of cash flow volatility and the maintenance of quality staff more challenging. Tokenizing tourism assets would, therefore, help alleviate the financial burdens of seasonal business.

The extent of what can be tokenized in the tourism and hospitality sector may depend on the size, type, and uniqueness of the product or assets in question. These may range from a hotel or restaurant to a world heritage site, an artifact in a museum, cities as attractions, and art. Destinations that are not easily accessible yet have unique tourism products to offer could also develop new business models designed around a digital transformation strategy whereby they can be part of the real or virtual consumption of their products. By doing so, they will be in a position to not only sustain their business but also create additional streams of revenue.

Limitations and Further Research

There are also challenges regarding the tokenization of tourism assets. The first is the adoption of blockchain technology by the industry. Although Bitcoin and blockchain technology have been around since 2009, research into their applications beyond cryptocurrencies is nascent and the technology is constantly evolving. Therefore, research including applied case studies would be of enormous value for the tourism industry. Another concern is fostering a sense of community via blockchains. The participants of a blockchain need to agree to be on it and still need a sufficient amount of technical understanding before using it. Further research on this topic will allow us to develop practical solutions that industry practitioners can also implement.

Another concern related to blockchain technology is its high-energy consumption for certain types of public and permissionless blockchains. Climate change and sustainability are increasingly prescient concerns and the high-energy consumption of this technology is one of the reasons delaying its wider adoption. Several cryptocurrencies are based on the proof of work (PoW) mechanism, which enables reaching a majority consensus on the blockchain by using computing power. However, there are other consensus mechanisms available such as proof of stake (PoS), which is energy-efficient for large-scale systems (Sedlmeir et al., 2020). Furthermore, carbon offset can be added to the prices (like airplane tickets) of NFTs and other tokens, which would help diminish the environmental concerns. Thus, leadership in tourism technology adoption promises to be the way of the future (Spencer et al., 2012).

Technology can help alleviate the consequences of COVID-19 for the tourism industry. According to Sigala (2020), technology is the heart of the revitalizing process of tourism after COVID-19. In addition to the traditional way of doing business, the tourism industry needs to think outside of the proverbial box and understand the new technologies of blockchain and tokenization and their practical applications. The application of these technologies to the tourism industry is a viable option for sustainable financial gain as shown in this study. If the tourism industry and its related research streams are to move forward from COVID-19's financial stress, innovative ways of using technology in the tourism industry must be investigated. Until now, most of the research about COVID-19 and tourism has examined the pandemic's economic and social impacts on consumers. It is also essential to change our perspective regarding tourism revenues and understand that blockchain can provide this via tokenized tourism assets.

Future studies are needed to investigate other uses of NFTs and tokenization processes from different perspectives toward overcoming the social, economic, and environmental challenges of tourism destinations.

References

Abrate, G., Bruno, C., Erbetta, F., & Fraquelli, G. (2020). Which future for traditional travel agencies? A dynamic capabilities approach. *Journal of Travel Research, 59*(5), 777–791. https://doi.org/10.1177/0047287519870250.

Adele (2021, December 9). Hospitality industry NFTs will be the next big thing in 2022 - Marriott's VP agrees. NFT Evening. Retrieved from: https://nftevening.com/hospitality-industry-nfts-will-be-the-next-big-thing-in-2022-marriotts-vp-agrees/.

Assaf, A. G., Kock, F., & Tsionas, M. (2022). Tourism during and after COVID-19: An expert-informed agenda for future research. *Journal of Travel Research, 61*(2), 454–457.

Burks, Z. 2021. You can now purchase NFTs with a credit card on Mintable! *Medium.* https://mintable.medium.com/you-can-now-purchase-nfts-with-a-credit-card-on-mintable-71451379f453

Clark, M. (2021, March 8). The brands are at it again—Taco Bell is hopping on the NFT train. The Verge. https://www.theverge.com/2021/3/8/22319868/taco-bell-nfts-gif-tacos-sell.

Camisón, C., Puig-Denia, A., Forés, B., Fabra, M. E., Muñoz, A., & Munoz Martinez, C. (2016). The importance of internal resources and capabilities and destination resources to explain firm competitive position in the Spanish tourism industry. *International Journal of Tourism Research, 18*(4), 341–356.

Duarte Alonso, A., Kok, S., & O'Shea, M. (2021). Peru's emerging craft-brewing industry and its implications for tourism. *International Journal of Tourism Research, 23*(3), 319–331.

Goanta, C. (2020). Selling LAND in Decentraland: The regime of non-fungible tokens on the Ethereum blockchain under the digital content directive. In Lehavi, A., & Levine-Schnur, R. (eds.), *Disruptive Technology, Legal Innovation, and the Future of Real Estate*, 139–154. Cham: Springer. https://doi.org/10.1007/978-3-030-52387-9_8

Iansiti, M., & Lakhani, K. R. (2017). The truth about blockchain. *Harvard Business Review, 95*(1), 118–127.

Jiang, Y., Ritchie, B. W., & Verreynne, M. L. (2022). A resource-based typology of dynamic capability: Managing tourism in a turbulent environment. *Journal of Travel Research, 61*(5), 1006–1023.

Laurent, P., Chollet, T., Burke, M., & Seers, T. (2018). The tokenization of assets is disrupting the financial industry. Are you ready. *Inside Magazine, 19*, 62–67.

Önder, I., & Gunter, U. (2022). Blockchain: Is it the future for the tourism and hospitality industry? *Tourism Economics, 28*(2), 291–299.

Önder, I., & Treiblmaier, H. 2018. Blockchain and tourism: Three research propositions. *Annals of Tourism Research, 72*(Sep.): 180–182. https://doi.org/10.1016/j.annals.2018.03.005

Ozdemir, A. I., Ar, I. M., & I. Erol. 2020. Assessment of blockchain applications in travel and tourism industry. *Quality & Quantity, 54*(5): 1549–1563. https://doi.org/10.1007/s11135-019-00901-w

Pillai, R., & Sivathanu, B. (2020). Adoption of AI-based chatbots for hospitality and tourism. *International Journal of Contemporary Hospitality Management, 32*(10), 3199–3226.

Rashideh, W. (2020). Blockchain technology framework: Current and future perspectives for the tourism industry. *Tourism Management, 80*, 104125.

Rejeb, A., Keogh, J. G., & Treiblmaier, H. (2020). How blockchain technology can benefit marketing: Six pending research areas. *Frontiers in Blockchain, 3*, 1–12.

Rogers, E. M. 2003. *Diffusion of Innovations, 5th Edition* (5th ed.). Free Press.

Rosenblatt, K. (2021, November 2). The McRib is back at McDonald's. It's also an NFT. NBC News. https://www.nbcnews.com/pop-culture/pop-culture-news/mcrib-back-mcdonalds-a lso-nft-rcna4277.

Sedlmeir, J., Buhl, H. U., Fridgen, G., & Keller, R. (2020). The energy consumption of blockchain technology: Beyond myth. *Business & Information Systems Engineering, 62*(6), 599–608.

Sigala, M. (2020). Tourism and COVID-19: Impacts and implications for advancing and resetting industry and research. *Journal of Business Research, 117*, 312–321.

Soulard, J., McGehee, N. G., & Stern, M. (2019). Transformative tourism organizations and glocalization. *Annals of Tourism Research, 76*, 91–104.

Spencer, A. J., Buhalis, D., & Moital, M. (2012). A hierarchical model of technology adoption for small owner-managed travel firms: An organizational decision-making and leadership perspective. *Tourism Management, 33*(5), 1195–1208.

Teece, D. J., Pisano, G., & Shuen, A. (1997). Dynamic capabilities and strategic management. *Strategic Management Journal, 18*(7), 509–533.

Treiblmaier, H. (2021). The token economy as a key driver for tourism: Entering the next phase of blockchain research. *Annals of Tourism Research, 91*, 103177.

Venkatesh, V., Morris, M. G., Davis, G. B., & Davis, F. D. (2003). User acceptance of information technology: Toward a unified view. *MIS Quarterly, 27*(3), 425–478. https://doi.org/10.2307/30036540

Wernerfelt, B. (1984). A resource-based view of the firm. *Strategic Management Journal, 5*(2), 171–180.

Wöber, K., & Gretzel, U. (2000). Tourism managers' adoption of marketing decision support systems. *Journal of Travel Research, 39*(2), 172–181.

6

REVOLUTIONIZING TOURISM PAYMENTS

The Formation of Decentralized Tourism Financial Systems

Seda Karagoz Zeren

Introduction

Tourism is a huge industry that generates billions of dollars each year. Travel and tourism have always made a significant contribution to the global economy, with millions of people traveling to various destinations around the world each year. Traveling to new places and exploring different cultures is an exciting and enriching experience. The world of tourism is constantly evolving with new technologies and innovations changing the way we travel and experience new destinations. From booking flights to booking accommodation, technology has revolutionized the way we travel. However, the payment process has remained largely unchanged so far. Despite the growth of the industry, the payment systems used by most tourism companies have remained relatively unchanged. Traditional payment systems have become centralized, slow, and expensive, and the need for revolutionary change is long overdue. Traditional payment methods used in the tourism industry are often slow, expensive, insecure, and inconvenient for travelers. They pose many inconveniences to existing payment systems, from high transaction fees to long processing times. Traditional payment systems are often subject to high fees, exchange rates, and security risks. The disruption of traditional payment systems and the increasing digitalization of the world are also changing the way we pay for our travel experiences. Traditional payment methods like credit cards and cash transactions have been the norm for years, but with the rise of decentralized financial systems, the game is about to change. This is where decentralized financial systems come in. Decentralized finance (DeFi) is a term used to describe a new financial system built on blockchain technology that operates without the need for intermediaries such as banks. One of the most exciting developments in this area has been the rise of decentralized financial systems that have revolutionized the way tourists pay for their trips. With the advent of blockchain

DOI: 10.4324/9781003351917-6

technology and cryptocurrencies, travelers now have more options than ever to pay for their trips. Powered by blockchain technology, these systems offer a secure, fast, and cost-effective way for tourists to make payments without the need for intermediaries such as banks. This means that tourists can have more control over their finances, avoid high transaction fees, and benefit from faster payment processing times. Decentralized financial systems offer several benefits, such as lower transaction fees, faster transaction times, and increased security. They also offer greater privacy and control over personal data, making it a game-changer for travelers who value their security and independence. This innovative payment system is set to revolutionize the tourism industry by offering travelers faster, cheaper, and safer payment options. Decentralization eliminates the need for third-party intermediaries, providing a more secure and efficient payment system. Blockchain technology enables transactions to be completed immediately and at a cheaper cost, which is advantageous for both the customer and the company. This revolution in tourism payments not only simplifies the process for travelers but also creates new opportunities for small businesses and local economies. This is just the beginning of the future of tourism payments, with new technologies and innovations being developed every day. As the tourism industry continues to evolve, it is essential to stay up to date with the latest changes and developments to ensure businesses remain competitive and consumers have the best possible experience. Whether you are a frequent traveler or a travel industry professional, it is essential to understand the implications of these changes and how they will shape the future of tourism.

In this chapter, we will explore the future of tourism payments and how localization has played an important role in this change. From faster, safer transactions to greater financial inclusion, we'll take a closer look at the benefits and challenges of decentralized payments in the tourism industry. It is the purpose of this chapter to explore the impact of decentralized financial systems on the tourism industry, how they have changed the way payments are made, and what awaits the industry in the future as these systems continue to evolve. For this purpose, first of all, the decentralized finances are examined and the effects of these transactions on the tourism sector are presented under the main headings.

Decentralized Finance (DeFi)

DeFi stands for decentralized finance and is an ecosystem where financial transactions are made without the need for a central authority. DeFi is a financial system that disables traditional financial institutions and intermediaries. DeFi makes it possible to carry out financial transactions directly between two parties using blockchain technology. DeFi is a financial system that does not need a central authority or intermediaries like traditional financial instruments and services. Using innovative technologies such as smart contracts built on blockchain technology, this system provides a financial system that is open to everyone's participation and that anyone can directly control. This system allows users to control their assets and perform financial transactions without the need for any intermediary institution.

This allows us to get rid of many of the constraints of traditional finance. Instead of replacing traditional financial institutions, DeFi creates an entirely new financial ecosystem. DeFi operates using open-source software protocols with no centralized management structure. These protocols allow users to directly store, borrow, lend, and trade assets using a special type of computer program known as smart contracts. DeFi is also open source, meaning anyone can review and improve the code. The basic philosophy of decentralized finance is the elimination of centralized structures in financial transactions. In this way, financial transactions can be carried out faster, cheaper, and more securely. The core principles of DeFi include everyone's accessibility, transparency, smart contracts, and the use of blockchain technology. Thanks to blockchain technology, all transactions are recorded and verified and therefore safe, reliable, and traceable. DeFi is an important part of the cryptocurrency ecosystem and has many different applications. These applications include currencies, lending, borrowing, exchanges, insurance, liquidity pools, and other financial instruments. These applications are explicitly recorded on the blockchain and the agreements between the parties are carried out directly. By deploying Ethereum smart contracts, DeFi developers can launch decentralized applications (dapps) that work exactly as scheduled and are available to anyone with an internet connection. In a smart contract, the entire contract is specified as part of the computer program and is stored on a blockchain. The program includes the terms of the loan and the specific actions it will take based on compliance (for example, the transfer of collateral ownership in the event of default). There is no need to involve parties besides the borrower and the lender because the blockchain ensures faithful implementation of the contract (Andolfatto & Martin, 2022). DeFi applications can be built on different networks, such as Binance Smart Chain (BNB Chain Documentation, 2022), Tron (Tron Whitepaper, 2018), Polkadot (Wood, 2023), and NEO (NEO Whitepaper, 2023), even though they are based on Ethereum smart contracts. The lack of a central party acting as an intermediary party in transactions characterizes these networks as a whole.

The historical development of decentralized finance was described by Zetzsche, Arner, and Buckley (2020) as the transformation of services provided by traditional financial institutions into a decentralized structure with technology as a result of the transformation of centralized financial institutions into local, regional, and global access points as well as the regulations and regulations experienced in the services provided (Zetzsche et al., 2020).

The existence of a decentralized financial system becomes a priority as a result of the problems experienced at the point of access to the service during central financial transactions. Especially in developing and underdeveloped countries, various problems can be experienced in financial transactions. For example, restrictions on users' access to financial centers (limited access to ATMs, banks, etc.), complex presentation of financial transactions for users, and loss of cost and time in financial transactions (transactions taken by financial institutions in banking transactions such as Swift, EFT, and Remittance). Decentralized presentation of financial transactions has come to the fore due to reasons such as fees and the transfer of these transactions to the relevant accounts after certain periods. FinTech, which refers to the technical management of financial services in decentralized finance transactions, and RegTech, which refers to the technical management of financial regulatory transactions, take place together (Anagnostopoulos, 2018). While many DeFi applications emerged as a result of FinTech and DeFi working together, RegTech is used to manage regulatory requirements regarding the use of DeFi and FinTech. There are four basic technologies in DeFi transactions. These are artificial intelligence, blockchain (including distributed ledgers and smart contracts), cloud, and data. Another classification is artificial intelligence, big data, cloud, and DLT (including blockchain and smart contracts) technology (Zetzsche et al., 2020).

One of the biggest advantages of decentralized finance is that in the absence of a central authority, transactions can be carried out quickly, cost-effectively, and transparently. Therefore, DeFi has great potential for financial inclusion by facilitating access to financial services for people who do not have access to the financial system. DeFi constitutes one of the most important uses for public blockchains. In DeFi, a method that measures the value of all assets locked in DeFi protocols along with the transaction volumes performed on crypto exchanges in March 2020, the total value locked (TVL) in DeFi protocols has been measured at over $800 million (Huilgolkar, 2020; Schmidt, 2021). On the 27th of March, 2023, this growth value was $49.73 billion according to "DeFiLlama" (Akhlaghi, 2023; DeFiLlama, 2023). Figure 2.1 shows the value of total assets in DeFi protocols.

In DeFi projects, financial investment specialists evaluate projects on the basis of market value, trading volume, and locked-in value (TVL), excluding total and circulating supply, to measure the performance of the investment. In this respect, as seen in Figure 6.1, the total locked value of DeFi projects increases and decreases in various periods between 2021 and 2023. With the impact of technology and the presence of current developments, DeFi projects in financial markets will also try to maintain their sustainability. The grouping of DeFi projects selected based on their locked total value as per blockchain protocols in 2022 is shown in Figure 6.2.

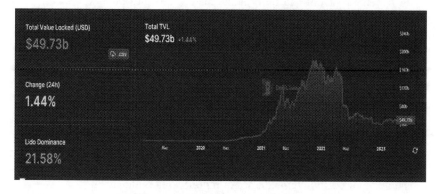

FIGURE 6.1   DeFi – total value locked 2023 (USD) (DeFiLlama, 2023).

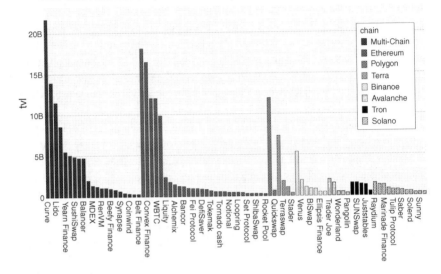

FIGURE 6.2 Total value locked 2022 (USD) (Meister & Price, 2022, p. 4).

When Figure 6.2 is examined, it is seen that DeFi protocols created on multiple platforms, which are grouped as multi-chain most, are followed by protocols created on the Ethereum network. In March 2023, it is seen that the distribution of these protocols consists of DeFi projects created with protocols grouped as multi-chain, followed by Ethereum protocols. Table 6.1 shows the top ten rankings in DeFi projects by TVL in 2023. It is seen that the DeFi project named "Curve," which has the most locked total value in 2022, took fourth place in 2023, while the project named "Lido" ranked first. Multi-chain platforms were used to create two projects in different years at the top of the list. It can be mentioned that the total locked value of projects in which platforms are used together in DeFi projects to be created based on this issue may be higher than projects using a single platform.

The benefits of DeFi can be broadly categorized into three key areas: insecure infrastructure, unauthorized innovation, and community-driven governance (Makarov & Schoar, 2022; OECD, 2022):

- Insecure infrastructure means that all transactions in the DeFi ecosystem are carried out on the Ethereum blockchain, which is immutable and transparent. This means users can be assured that their money is safe and will remain accessible even if a particular dapp or service is offline.
- Unauthorized innovation refers to the fact that anyone can create a dapp on the Ethereum platform. This open-source development model enables rapid innovation and keeps the playing field level for all participants. It also means that there is no need for costly intermediaries or rent-seeking middlemen.

TABLE 6.1 DeFi – total locked value (2023) (DeFiLlama, 2023)

DeFi project	Chains	TVL ($) in billion
Lido	Five chains (Ethereum, Solana, Moonbeam, Moonriver, Terra Classic)	10.7
MakerDAO	One chain (Ethereum)	7.59
AAVE	Seven chains (Ethereum, Polygon, Avalanche, Arbitrum, Optimism, Fantom, Harmony)	5.44
Curve	Twelve chains (Ethereum, Polygon, Arbitrum, Optimism, Fantom, Celo, Avalanche, Gnosis, Kava, Moonbeam, Aurora, Harmony)	4.65
Uniswap	Six chains (Ethereum, Polygon, Arbitrum, Optimism, BSC, Celo)	3.93
JustLend	One chain (Tron)	3.73
Convex Finance	Three chains (Ethereum, Arbitrum, Polygon)	3.72
PankaceSwap	Three chains (BSC, Aptos, Ethereum)	2.48
Coinbase Wrapped Staked ETH	One chain (Ethereum)	2.13
Instadapp	One chain (Ethereum)	2.06

- Community-driven governance is a key advantage of the DeFi ecosystem. Since all decisions are taken by consensus among stakeholders, there is no central authority that dictates terms or imposes fees. This decentralization also makes it much more difficult for bad actors to take control of the system or manipulate it for their benefit.

Additionally, since smart contracts handle all transactions in DeFi and no central authority verifies the contractors' identities, there is no need for personal data. There are no security issues, and managing sensitive data doesn't require an external server (Caldarelli & Ellul, 2021).

One of DeFi's most popular applications is liquidity pools, which are used to provide liquidity. These pools allow users to accumulate their assets in the pool and exchange them with other assets in the pool. In this way, a system that is more resistant to price fluctuations is formed. However, DeFi is not yet as common or user-friendly as traditional financial instruments, and it has risks. Smart contracts in DeFi transactions need reliable data sources (databases, sensors, or other smart contracts). Data feeders report off-chain data to an on-chain system (Aspembitova & Bentley, 2022). DeFi protocols have several advantages, but they also have some drawbacks. Table 6.2 displays these benefits and restrictions.

Decentralized financial transactions can also be used in the tourism sector, where financial transactions are carried out, as it saves time and money, and

TABLE 6.2 Advantages and disadvantages of DeFi (Stepanova & Eriņš, 2021, p. 332)

Advantages	Disadvantages
• The use of digital technologies • Elimination of control from large financial institutions • Accessibility of financial services • Privacy • Open software code • Passive income • Lower transaction costs	• Information shortage • Lack of legal framework • Lack of support • Hacker attacks

provides reliability and transparency in transactions. Determining the effects of decentralized financial transactions in the tourism sector first requires defining existing financial payment systems in the industry and examining how decentralized financial transactions can alleviate the issues these traditional financial payment systems encounter.

Decentralized Financial Transactions in the Tourism Sector

The tourism sector is an industry consisting of a wide range of activities. For this reason, the financial information of the sector may change and this information generally changes according to companies or fields of activity. The financial payment system in tourism is a system that enables customers to make their payments easily and safely in the tourism sector. Thanks to this system, tourism businesses can receive their customers' payments quickly and easily and increase customer satisfaction. This system covers the payment methods used by tourists when purchasing tourism services such as accommodation, transportation, food and beverage, and tours.

Traditional financial payment systems consist of three main elements and processes (Gogoski, 2012, pp. 438–439):

- Payment instruments that are a means of authorizing and sending payment (means by which the payer authorizes funds to be transferred to his bank, or by which the payee instructs his bank for funds to be collected from the payer).
- The transaction (including clearing) involving the exchange of the payment order between the relevant banks (and accounts).
- A settlement instrument for the banks involved (the payer's bank must reimburse the creditor's bank bilaterally or through accounts, the two banks hold at a third-party settlement agency).

According to the demand congruence theory, industries will need more sources of finance to accelerate the expansion of the financial system, and in this process, the industrial structure will rise due to capital accumulation (Patrick, 1966).

At the same time, a new method of financing is urgently needed to make financial structures and derivatives more diverse to expand the scale and increase efficiency (Rajan & Zingales, 2001). Especially with the effect of the pandemic process and the presence of technology, this financing method has transformed from a centralized structure to a decentralized structure.

The growth of the tourism industry is a dynamic process that is essentially supported by financial systems and consists of appearance, production, and development (Cui, 2017). The increase in tourism encourages the development of the financial system. To meet the demands of more and more customers in the current internet age, an increasing number of tourism businesses and the government are launching electronic tickets, online banking services, electronic payments, travel cards, tourism credit cards, and insurance (Liao et al., 2018).

Financial payment systems in the tourism sector make tourists feel more comfortable and safe in their travels. It is also important for tourism businesses because the correct and reliable management of payment transactions is important for the financial health of the business. In the tourism industry, financial payment systems are methods used to pay for travel and vacation plans. These systems are used by travel agencies, hotels, airlines, car rental companies, and other tourism service providers. Traditionally, payment methods such as cash, credit cards, and bank transfers have been used in the tourism industry. However, in recent years, digital payment systems, especially mobile payments, have also become popular in the tourism industry.

The financial payment systems used in the tourism sector are given as follows:

- **Credit cards**: Credit cards from Mastercard, Visa, and American Express are frequently used by tourism companies.
- **Bank transfers**: Tourism companies allow customers to transfer funds directly to their bank accounts.
- **PayPal**: Digital payment platforms such as PayPal are used by tourism companies to make payments to customers.
- **Mobile payments**: Mobile payment platforms such as Apple Pay, Google Pay, and Samsung Pay are used by tourism companies to make payments to customers.
- **Cryptocurrencies**: Some tourism companies allow customers to pay with cryptocurrencies.

Tourism companies use reliable payment systems to ensure that customers have a safe and fast payment experience. These systems also allow customers to easily process payments and make it easier for tourism companies to monitor their financial transactions. These systems have been extended from centralized financial payment systems to decentralized financial payment systems. One of the best examples of this is that travel and tourism agencies can make reservations with cryptocurrencies.

DeFi can be used in many different ways in tourism businesses. For example, a tourism business might create its decentralized finance application to receive payments from its customers. This app provides verification and recording of payments using blockchain technology. In this way, the business can receive payments more quickly and securely and manage its financial transactions more transparently. In addition, tourism businesses can directly transact with other businesses using decentralized finance applications. In this way, tourism businesses can perform their transactions more quickly and cheaply and reduce their costs by using fewer intermediaries in their financial transactions. DeFi makes it possible to provide many financial services, such as payment, lending, insurance, and wealth management, to tourism businesses. In this way, tourism businesses can make their financial transactions more secure, transparent, and automated. For example, a tourism business can pay its customers through a blockchain-based platform, or an insurance company can automatically process its customers' insurance claims using blockchain technology. In this way, financial transactions become faster and safer, while the costs and delays that may arise from the transactions of intermediary institutions can be reduced.

Research on the use of cryptocurrency and blockchain technology in financial payment systems in the tourism sector is increasing. The number of documents published on this subject has increased by an average of 23% annually. This ratio was created in the Web of Science (WoS) Core Collection and Clarivate Analytics data formula on March 16, 2023. All indexed articles containing the following keywords in the 2018–2023 period:

> Blockchain (BC) and tourism; cryptocurrencies (CC) and tourism; blockchain and hospitality; cryptocurrencies (CC) and hospitality; blockchain (BC) and tourism and hospitality; cryptocurrencies (CC) and tourism and hospitality; blockchain (BC) and cryptocurrencies (CC) and tourism and hospitality; decentralized finance and tourism; decentralized finance and hospitality; decentralized finance and tourism and hospitality; decentralized finance and blockchain (BC) and cryptocurrencies (CC) and tourism and hospitality

have been selected. A total of 69 documents have been investigated. Table 6.3 shows the number of publications by keywords and years. Published posts are only shown when relevant keywords are selected. When other keywords are searched, they are not included in the table because no publication can be found.

Formula (6.1) is given as follows:

$$r = \left(\frac{x(t)}{x(0)} \right)^{\frac{1}{t}} - 1 \tag{6.1}$$

where $x(t)$ is the final value, $x(0)$ is the initial value, and t is the time in years.

TABLE 6.3 Number of publications-related keywords

Year	Number of publications – keywords				Total	Yearly growth rate (%)
	BC and tourism	CC and tourism	BC and hospitality	BC and tourism and hospitality		
2018	1	–	1	–	2	–
2019	7	1	1	2	11	450.00
2020	14	1	2	3	20	81.82
2021	13	–	–	–	12	−35.00
2022	14	2	–	–	16	23.08
2023	2	–	4	1	7	−56.25
Total	51	4	8	6	69	23.21[a]

[a] The annual average publication rate between 2018 and 2023 is calculated with Formula (6.1).

Barrutia Barreto, Urquizo Maggia, and Acevedo (2019) state that the use of cryptocurrencies in financial payments should be expanded due to the high tourism potential of Latin America and the Caribbean, and that governments should support micro-tourism businesses with Initial Coin Offerings (ICO) (Barrutia Barreto et al., 2019). Tham and Sigala (2020) critically examine the use of cryptocurrencies and blockchain from the perspective of sustainable tourism (Tham & Sigala, 2020). Onder and Treiblmaier (2018) state that blockchain technology in tourism can be used in online evaluations, and cryptocurrencies can be used to create a new market and in tourism transactions without intermediaries (Onder & Treiblmaier, Blockchain and tourism: three research propositions, 2018). Hendry and McGhee (2018) give the example of the creation of an ICO to develop a resort on Great Keppel Island in the Great Barrier Reef off the Queensland coast, where cryptocurrencies and blockchain technology are used for financial payments in tourism (Hendry & McGhee, 2018). Another example is expressed by Karagoz Zeren and Demirel (2020) as the use of cryptocurrencies in the customer loyalty card program of Singapore Airlines, which is an airline (Karagöz Zeren & Demirel, 2020). Other examples of blockchain-based applications in tourism are the "Dubai Smart Tourism 2.0" project and the applications created by the "CoolCousin travel company" (Bodkhe et al., 2019, August). Onder and Gunter (2022) present their ideas about the future of blockchain technology in tourism with the COVID-19 outbreak (Onder & Gunter, Blockchain: is it the future for the tourism and hospitality industry? 2022). Jain et al. (2023) examine the academic studies on the use of blockchain technology in tourism with a systematic literature review. They analyze academic publications in two groups, thematically and methodologically, and group publications in tourism within the thematic group under the headings of "Smart Tourism, Tourism Destination Focused, Traveler Focused, Digital Payments, Token Economy, and Implementation and Adoption" (Jain et al., 2023).

The increase in decentralized financial payment transactions in tourism is seen with the quantitative increase of the relevant articles and the existence of applications. For this reason, it is necessary to present practical solutions to theoretical studies on how decentralized financial payment systems can be used in tourism enterprises. In the next section, the infrastructure of the financial payment system, which can be experienced in a tourism business, in the form of a decentralized structure (DeFi) project is presented as a proposal.

The Architecture of Decentralized Tourism Financing Systems

Five fundamental layers define the underlying data structure, storage structure, and ledger model of blockchain as a theoretical basis. Technically, these layers consist of the data layer, network layer, consensus layer, contract layer, and application layer. This layer of information is shown in Figure 6.3.

The data layer is the layer that contains data information based on the blockchain. In this layer, there are transactions, blocks, Hash function, Merkle tree, and the digital signature within the data structure, storage structure, and ledger patterns (Uddin et al., 2021). In the network layer, it is the structure in which peer-to-peer blockchain nodes are established to create the decentralized structure that forms the basis of this section. Decentralization means that blockchain nodes are peer-to-peer at the physical level, and each node can communicate with the other without switching (Deng et al., 2023). The consensus layer, however, is a layer that forms the core of blockchain protocols. Behind every blockchain is a consensus algorithm. The consensus layer is the most critical layer for any blockchain (Ethereum, Hyperledger, or others). Consensus is responsible for validating the blocks, sorting the blocks, and ensuring that everyone agrees on them (Packt, 2023). Consensus and contract

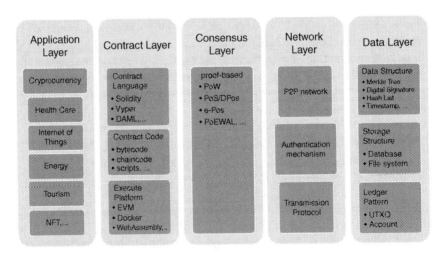

FIGURE 6.3 Blockchain architecture.

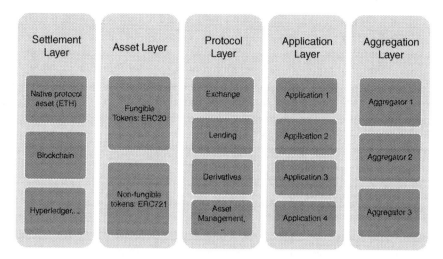

FIGURE 6.4   DeFi structure.

layers include smart contracts, consensus protocols, and incentive mechanisms (Lu, 2019). The contract layer implements smart contracts, which are a set of digitally determined commitments that cannot be changed once deployed and are executed immediately after they are triggered. As an extension of the blockchain, smart contracts enable the blockchain to have the ability to manage logically complex transactions (Deng et al., 2023). The application layer contains the application software of the blockchain. It provides a human-readable interface where users can track their transactions (Sarmah, 2018). In the decentralized tourism financial system, a structure in which tourism transactions are carried out can be presented together with the blockchain technology (blockchain) layers. While creating blockchain protocols – Ethereum, Hyperledger, etc. – smart contracts can be created on platforms. The working principles of these platforms and the programming languages they use are different from each other. Smart contracts can be created with the use of the DeFi protocol that is desired to be created for the tourism business. For this, the layers required to create the DeFi protocol should be examined. DeFi uses a multi-layered architecture. Each layer has a separate purpose. The layers are built on top of each other, creating an open and highly composable infrastructure that allows anyone to build, reorganize, or use other parts of the stack (Schär, 2021). DeFi layers are shown in Figure 6.4.

The first layer, the settlement layer, consists of distributed ledger technology (DLT). DLT contains the hardware layer where a peer-to-peer computer network is required to calculate transactions and sequentially store them in a distributed database (Maia & Vieira dos Santos, 2022). A sort of digital infrastructure known as an asset layer makes it possible to manage, trade, and monitor digital assets like tokens, cryptocurrencies, and other representations of digital value. Any assets that have been issued on top of the settlement layer fall under this category. This contains all assets issued on this Blockchain, including the native protocol asset (usually referred to as tokens) (Fikri et al., 2022). DeFi protocols are made up of software that is built on top of the asset layer at the protocol level, where specific use cases are developed and implemented as several smart contracts that are carried out after the occurrence of specific circumstances (OECD, 2022). The protocol layer consists of the compiler and the ability to build application programming interfaces (APIs). A compiler is a program that converts existing high-level programming languages to low-level programming languages. At this layer, developers can write code, compile it to bytecode (machine language), and deploy it to DLT. Additionally, developers can create an API that will allow other developers to interact with the distributed code (Maia & Vieira dos Santos, 2022). Smart contracts and programming languages are part of this layer. The user-focused programs are housed in the application layer. Protocols are easy to use since smart contract interaction is typically described via a web browser-based frontend (Fikri et al., 2022). In addition to the application layer, there is the aggregate layer. Users-focused platforms connected to a variety of applications and protocols are built by aggregators. They frequently give customers the ability to assess and compare services, conduct difficult operations by connecting to multiple protocols at once, and compile pertinent data simply and understandably (Schär, 2021).

Framework structures can be developed from many tourism-related aspects to construct decentralized tourism finance systems. In this chapter, it is initially suggested that customers who wish to take advantage of the first frame structure in the tourism industry adopt a decentralized structure for their payment method. The formation of the contracts that must be made between the providers to the tourism industry is where another framework structure comes into play. Since similar application protocols and steps will be realized, the chapter only deals with the presentation of the smart contract protocol to be experienced between the customer and the provider requesting tourism service with DeFi protocol steps. These steps are shown in Figure 6.5.

In Figure 6.5, it is aimed to create a blockchain-based DeFi protocol for a service type determined by the customer who wants to benefit from a tourism service. For example, let this service protocol be executed between a customer who wants to stay in a hotel and the hotel management. In this case, the customer who wants to stay at the hotel is presented with a guest contract that includes the date, room conditions, accommodation style, payment method, and special conditions based on accommodation requirements. Information containing these conditions can be created as a smart contract using blockchain technology. In the creation of this smart contract, the DLT to be used must be selected first. Assuming that this technology is chosen as Ethereum, the settlement layer of the DeFi protocol, which is desired to be created in a decentralized tourism financial system, is created. Then, ERC-721 is created by choosing the cryptological encryption method, since it is desired to create a protocol that includes non-financial information in the

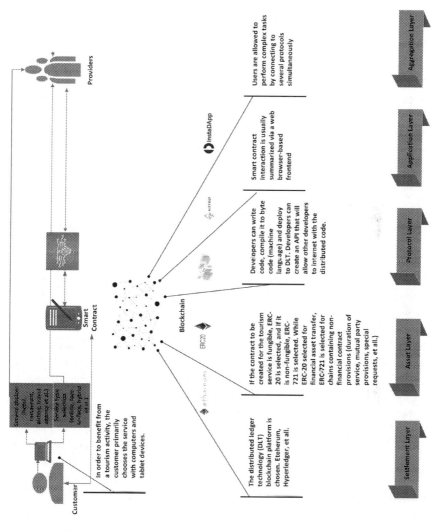

FIGURE 6.5 DeFi structure in tourism.

Ethereum protocol, which is the asset layer. The distributed ledger created in the protocol layer is programmed using the Solidity programming language with the Ethereum virtual machine, and an application is created in the application layer using the web browser. Finally, the structure that provides the presentation of the user interface and creates the application protocol can be presented between the reciprocal parties. In this case, when the parties perform their transactions within this application interface since all data will be located on a blockchain base, transactions are approved without the need for a third agent and without any abuse and interference.

The example presented for the structure of the decentralized tourism financial system can be generalized and presented in a structure that includes all tourism stakeholders. In this example, the smart contract protocol to be established between customer-hotel management is similar between hotel management-supplier/ manufacturer, airline-travel agency, travel agency-customer, customer-airline enterprise, hotel management-central administrations, public administration-related organizations, and so on can also be installed.

Conclusion and Discussion

Developments in blockchain technology create differences in traditional payment systems, business processes, and management processes. The advantages and difficulties that these differences will create should also be evaluated in terms of the tourism sector. In this research, a proposal is presented that there can be decentralized financial payment systems in tourism financial payment systems and that decentralized financial protocols called DeFi can be used in tourism. A proposal has been made for presenting the contract and service confirmation between a customer who wants to benefit from a tourism business and the accommodation business as smart contracts, and presenting a decentralized financial payment system as a payment method. These protocols can then be developed among tourism stakeholders and integrated into the entire tourism sector. In the creation of the smart contract between the parties, especially in the choice of the payment method, the DeFi protocol steps, which are the settlement, asset, protocol, application, and aggregation layers, are also examined. In this chapter, it has also been determined that there are quantitative increases in academic publications about decentralized technologies in tourism. With this increase, it can be said that academic publications in tourism are suitable for this trend. Bodkhe et al. (2019) examine case studies of the existence of a system created with smart contracts and the use of blockchain technology in tourism and hospitality management in their academic publication. The book chapter proposal presented with the Blockchain architecture structure also supports the structure we have presented using the DeFi architecture structure. This system provides direct interaction between the parties in the tourism industry. All financial transactions between travel agencies, hotels, tour operators, and tourists can be carried out securely and quickly thanks to blockchain technology. The decentralized tourism financial system offers a more transparent, secure, and cost-effective alternative to financial transactions. This system can also reduce transaction times and costs by enabling transactions between parties in the tourism industry to be processed quickly. Among the limitations of the decentralized tourism financial payment system are the structural challenges presented by this technology. The fact that it requires superior programming language knowledge and the inadequacy of the existence of voluntary tourism enterprises in the implementation of this structure can also be among the limitations. Since the book chapter is a proposal for the creation of a decentralized tourism financial payment system, studies on the implementation of this proposal and the results of its implementation can be examined in future publications.

References

Akhlaghi, R. (2023, 03 07). *The evolution of DeFi and the emergence of DeFi derivatives.* (CoinDesk) Retrieved 03 15, 2023, from https://www.coindesk.com/coindesk-indices/2023/03/02/the-evolution-of-defi-and-the-emergence-of-defi-derivatives/.

Anagnostopoulos, I. (2018). Fintech and regtech: Impact on regulators and banks. *Journal of Economics and Business, 100,* 7–25.

Andolfatto, D., & Martin, F. M. (2022). The blockchain revolution: Decoding digital currencies. *Federal Reserve Bank of St. Louis Review, 104*(3), 149–165.

Aspembitova, A. T., & Bentley, M. A. (2022). Oracles in decentralized finance: Attack costs, profits and mitigation measures. *Entropy, 25*(1), 60.

Barrutia Barreto, I., Urquizo Maggia, J., & Acevedo, S. (2019). Criptomonedas y blockchain en el turismo como estrategia para reducir la pobreza. *RETOS. Revista de Ciencias de la Administración y Economía, 9*(18), 287–302.

BNB Chain Documentation. (2022, 03 16). *BNB chain: An ecosystem of blockchains.* Retrieved from https://docs.bnbchain.org/docs/overview.

Bodkhe, U., Bhattacharya, P., Tanwar, S., Tyagi, S., Kumar, N., & Obaidat, M. (2019, 08). BloHosT: Blockchain enabled smart tourism and hospitality management. *2019 international conference on computer, information and telecommunication systems (CITS)* (pp. 1–5). IEEE.

Caldarelli, G., & Ellul, J. (2021). The blockchain oracle problem in decentralized finance—A multivocal approach. *Applied Sciences, 11*(16), 7572.

Cui, P. (2017). On the coupling development of tourism growth and urbanization from the perspective of industry generation-A case study of Zhangjiajie. *Journal of Southwest University, 39*(12), 90–97.

DeFiLlama. (2023, 03 14). *Total value locked (USD).* Retrieved from https://defillama.com.

Deng, W., Huang, T., & Wang, H. (2023). A review of the key technology in a blockchain building decentralized trust platform. *Mathematics, 11*(101), 1–29.

Fikri, N., Rida, M., Abghour, N., Moussaid, K., El Omri, A., & Myara, M. (2022). A blockchain architecture for trusted sub-ledger operations and financial audit using decentralized microservices. *IEEE Access, 10,* 90873–90886.

Gogoski, R. (2012). Payment systems in economy-present end future tendencies. *Procedia-Social and Behavioral Sciences, 44,* 436–445.

Hendry, M., & McGhee, R. (2018, 09 04). *Cryptocurrency key to future on Great Barrier Reef island resort as developer looks for funding.* Retrieved 03 18, 2023, from https://

www.abc.net.au/news/2018-09-05/cryptocurrency-issued-to-fund-great-keppel-island-development/10199810.

Huilgolkar, H. (2020, 06 29). *Designing the most secure oracle for the Decentralized Finance*. (https://medium.com/) Retrieved 03 15, 2023, from https://medium.com/coinmonks/designing-the-most-secure-oracle-for-the-decentralized-finance-9853237f0c37.

Jain, P., Singh, R., Mishra, R., & Rana, N. (2023). Emerging dimensions of blockchain application in tourism and hospitality sector: A systematic literature review. *Journal of Hospitality Marketing & Management, 32*(4), 454–476.

Karagöz Zeren, S., & Demirel, E. (2020). Blockchain based smart contract applications in tourism industry. In U. Hacioglu (Ed.), *Digital business strategies in blockchain ecosystems. Contributions to management science* (pp. 601–615). Cham: Springer. https://doi.org/10.1007/9783030297398_28.

Liao, K., Yue, M., Sun, S., Xue, H., Liu, W., Tsai, S., & Wang, J. (2018). An evaluation of coupling coordination between tourism and finance. *Sustainability, 10*(2320), 1–23.

Lu, Y. (2019). The blockchain: State-of-the-art and research challenges. *Journal of Industrial Information Integration, 15*, 80–90.

Maia, G., & Vieira dos Santos, J. (2022). MiCA and DeFi ("Proposal for a Regulation on Market in Cryptoassets" and "Decentralised Finance"). *Revista Electronica de Direito, 2*(28), 57–82.

Makarov, I., & Schoar, A. (2022). *Cryptocurrencies and decentralized finance (DeFi)* (No. w30006). National Bureau of Economic Research.

Meister, B. K., & Price, H. C. (2022). Darwin among the cryptocurrencies. *arXiv preprint*, arXiv:2202.10340.

NEO Whitepaper. (2023, 03 16). Retrieved from https://docs.neo.org/v2/docs/en-us/basic/whitepaper.html.

OECD. (2022). *Why decentralised finance (DeFi) matters and the policy implications*. Retrieved from chrome-extension://efaidnbmnnnibpcajpcglclefindmkaj/https://www.oecd.org/daf/fin/financial-markets/Why-Decentralised-Finance-DeFi-Matters-and-the-Policy-Implications.pdf.

Onder, I., & Gunter, U. (2022). Blockchain: Is it the future for the tourism and hospitality industry? *Tourism Economics, 28*(2), 291–299.

Onder, I., & Treiblmaier, H. (2018). Blockchain and tourism: Three research propositions. *Annals of Tourism Research, 72*(C), 180–182.

Packt. (2023, 03 18). *Layered structure of the blockchain architecture*. (https://subscription.packtpub.com) Retrieved from https://subscription.packtpub.com/book/data/9781789804164/1/ch01lvl1sec07/layered-structure-of-the-blockchain-architecture.

Patrick, H. (1966). Financial development and economic growth in underdeveloped countries. *Economic Development and Cultural Change, 14*(2), 174–189.

Rajan, R., & Zingales, L. (2001). Financial systems, industrial structure, and growth. *Oxford Review of Economic Policy, 17*(4), 467–482.

Sarmah, S. (2018). Understanding blockchain technology. *Computer Science and Engineering, 8*(2), 23–29.

Schär, F. (2021). Decentralized finance: On blockchain-and smart contract-based financial markets. *Federal Reserve Bank of St. Louis Review, 103*(2), 154–174.

Schmidt, C. (2021). *DexGuru – real-time data, analytics and trading for AMMs in one place*. (www.defipulse.com) Retrieved from https://www.defipulse.com/blog/dexguru.

Stepanova, V., & Eriņš, I. (2021). Review of decentralized finance applications and their total value locked. *TEM Journal, 10*(1), 327–333.

Tham, A., & Sigala, M. (2020). Road block (chain): Bit (coin) s for tourism sustainable development goals? *Journal of Hospitality and Tourism Technology, 11*(2), 203–222.

Tron Whitepaper. (2018, 12 10). *Advanced decentralized blockchain platform.* Retrieved 03 16, 2023, from https://tron.network/static/doc/white_paper_v_2_0.pdf.

Uddin, M., Stranieri, A., Gondal, I., & Balasub, V. (2021). A survey on the adoption of blockchain in iot: Challenges and solutions. *Blockchain: Research and Applications, 2*(100006), 1–49.

Wood, G. (2023, 03 16). *Polkadot: Vision for a heterogeneous multi-chain framework.* Retrieved from https://www.semanticscholar.org/paper/POLKADOT%3A-VISION-FOR-A-HETEROGENEOUS-MULTI-CHAIN/f76f652385edc7f49563f77c12bbf28a990039cf.

Zetzsche, D. A., Arner, D. W., & Buckley, R. P. (2020). Decentralized finance. *Journal of Financial Regulation, 6*(2), 172–203.

7

UNLOCKING THE POTENTIAL OF BLOCKCHAIN TECHNOLOGY FOR MEDICAL TOURISM IN ALBANIA

Marc Pilkington and Erdita Kumaraku

Introduction

In this chapter, we set out to examine an emerging blockchain use case in an underexplored country and region of the world, namely medical tourism in the Republic of Albania, a small country populated by 2.845 million inhabitants (INSTAT, 2020), situated in the Western Balkans as well as a rising post-pandemic travel destination. In the first part, we provide a primer on a blockchain (also referred to as DLT hereafter) and medical tourism. Second, drawing on the first part, we propose a SWOT analysis of blockchain for medical tourism in Albania. Third, a questionnaire-based survey conducted on two distinct highly educated population subsets provides empirical support to our findings.

A Primer on Blockchain and Medical Tourism

Blockchain and Web 3.0

To define blockchain technology, it is best to begin with the idea of a shared, distributed, and encrypted database (Wright & De Filippi, 2015, p. 2; Pilkington, 2016). A blockchain is the processual outcome of a decentralized network, namely a chain of unalterable digital blocks containing information (e.g., timestamped transactions), a hash, and a hash of the previous block; it rests on a sophisticated consensus mechanism whereby transactions are audited and validated by the network without resorting to any central authority (Pilkington, 2016). Dogru et al. (2018) add the certification of the ownership status of assets, available to all network participants, to the list of applications of this decentralized protocol. The technology can create unique business opportunities in tourism. Blockchain tourism

DOI: 10.4324/9781003351917-7

use cases examined in the literature include loyalty programs and tokens (Dogru et al., 2018), smart contracts (Dogru et al., 2018; Microsoft, 2018), digital IDs and identification-related documents (e.g., birth certificates and driver's licenses; Amadeus IT Group, 2017), the tracking of the status and location of assets such as passenger bags or spare parts, the identity of crews and passengers, or contracts with other actors of the supply chain (IATA, 2018). Mofokeng and Fatima (2018) explore the potential of cryptocurrency payment systems for tourism growth. By certifying reviews, blockchain adds transparency and credibility to tourism platforms (Finyear, 2016). A proof-of-concept travel solution facilitating booking data processing was invented by Microsoft and Webjet (Microsoft, 2016).

Travelers looking for authenticity can monitor the food supply chain (Coleman, 2017; Önder & Gunter, 2022; Rizzo, 2017). Gamification is the process of layering game-like features onto a platform; combined with DLT and mobile services, it enables early-stage innovation and engagement in the creative process (Patrício et al., 2018). Destination marketing organizations and tourists can draw on gamified mobile experiences (Swacha, 2019). Focusing on the Republic of Moldova, Pilkington et al. (2017) explain that poverty alleviation and the fight against corruption through blockchain technology are part of the tourism 2.0 toolkit in developing countries. The shift from Web 1.0 to Web 2.0 was one from a static to a dynamic environment: "The beginning of the Web era, which then was mainly PC-based, enabled marketers to create static online brochures that later evolved into increasingly dynamic, multimedia resources" (Noti, 2013, p. 115). The first Web 2.0 conference was held on October 5–7, 2004, in San Francisco;[1] the term was coined by O'Reilly (30.9.2005) and heralded as a "business revolution in the computer industry caused by the move to the Internet as a platform, and an attempt to understand the rules for success on that new platform." Noti (2013, p. 116) explains that "with more Internet users accessing broadband and surfing the web at higher speeds, social networking, user-generated content, social bookmarking, sharing of information, videos, images, and opinions exponentially increased the amount of content on the Web." A third Internet revolution is underway today with the advent of Web 3.0, an umbrella term encompassing emerging technologies such as robotics, machine learning, virtual reality (the metaverse), and artificial intelligence, redefining the way economic agents interact, thereby defining new socioeconomic systems (Iansiti & Lakhani, 2017; Pilkington, 2022, p. 17).

Literature Review

Tourism in Albania

Historically, the Balkan region has been an important crossroad for different civilizations (Tamminen, 2004, p. 405). Tourism therein is not a new area of interest for scholars and policymakers. The Ministry of Tourism, Culture, Youth and Sport of Albania (2005) explains that Albania is a safe, high-value tourism destination featuring world-class natural and cultural attractions on a relatively small territory, within reach of European tourism markets. Marku (2014) and Ylli (2016) analyzed the Albanian national tourism strategy. Marku (2014, pp. 57–58) underlines in a rather poetic fashion the virgin nature and cultural wonders of Albania:

> From the crisp white snow of the mountains to the red fields of spring poppies, Albania's landscape is ever-changing with the seasons, offering visitors a warm summer beach holiday or a challenging mountain trek in the fall. In Albania, visitors are welcomed as guests as part of the country's rich cultural traditions and heritage. The warm hospitality of the Albanians will make everyone feel at home in this small wonderful land.

For Belegu (2021, pp. 3–4), Albania is a fast-changing country known for the beauty of its landscapes, price competitiveness, good customer care, multilingual skills, and hospitality. For Lubowiecki-Vikuk and Dryglas (2019, p. 1258), Albania is attractive due to her "favorable climate, beautiful and often pristine natural environment, a good position on the map of Europe, and competitive prices for international tourists." Recently, Menkshi et al. (2019) have focused on the great tourism development potential of the thermal springs of Benja-Albania.

Medical Tourism: A Rising Trend

In a globalized era, more patients seek treatment abroad for a fraction of the price in their home country. Over the last two decades, medical tourism, a high-potential niche market (Smith et al., 2011), has grown into an estimated $100 billion industry (Fetscherin & Stephano, 2016; Iordache et al., 2013) and has emerged as a powerful socio-economic force whereby citizens of developed countries in search of value (Deloitte Center for Health Solutions, 2017) bypass care offered at home and travel to less developed nations to receive a wide variety of medical services (Horowitz et al., 2007). The latter include preventive care, dental treatment, plastic surgery, aesthetic medicine dermatology, orthopedics, ophthalmology, gynecology, etc. (Beladi et al., 2015; Lunt et al., 2011), or even wellness facilities, such as spa centers (Quintela et al., 2016), thereby reflecting new patterns of consumption and production of healthcare services (Connell, 2013; Lunt et al., 2011). Weis et al. (2017) have analyzed new risks for patients associated with uninformed cost-effective medical choices, such as communication issues, endemic tropical diseases, unregulated hospitals, and organ trafficking. The lifting of travel restrictions in the aftermath of the COVID-19 pandemic has given a new impetus to medical tourism with increasing concerns for healthcare matters (Sun et al., 2022, p. 1).

Medical Tourism in the CEE and Albania

Lubowiecki-Vikuk and Kurkowiak (2017, p. 286) explain that academic research mainly focused on nations offering medical tourism services in Asia, the USA, and Central and South America in the early stages of industry growth. Yet some fast-changing and expanding regions, such as Central Eastern Europe (hereafter CEE), had been overlooked and poorly researched with few exceptions, such as Marinau et al. (2009), Kiss (2015), and Smith et al. (2016). More recently, Nexhipi (2018) and Belegu (2021) have produced relevant work with a narrower focus, respectively, on dental and medical tourism in Albania, which is our attention focus. Romaniuk and Szromek (2016) argue that Albania, Belarus, Moldova, and Ukraine were among the least performing at the macro-level, with minor improvements in recent years in CEE. He stated that quality, not price competitiveness, is the priority for medical tourism development. The assessment, however, needs to be more balanced. Albania and Moldova's health landscape has become polarized with several emerging high-quality private health providers, mostly in dental care and plastic surgery (see Table 7.1). As a matter of fact, in the year preceding the pandemic, it was estimated by Instat, the National Statistics Institute of Albania, in a comprehensive report titled "Tourism in numbers" that the number of medical tourists coming to Albania in 2020 would increase by around 15% from the previous year (Turizmi Në Shifra, 2019), a trend halted by the outbreak of the pandemic.

Medical Tourism and DLT (Distributed Ledger Technology)

DLT falls under the umbrella term of innovation. Yet when it comes to innovation in the tourism sector, Işık et al. (2022) distinguish between five classes: product innovation, service innovation, process innovation, management innovation, organizational innovation. Interestingly, as a foundational general-purpose technology, blockchain pervades these five classes. Existing DLT tourism use cases were sketched out in the introduction. Yet the intersection between DLT and medical tourism is narrower. The literature is recent; let us begin with a working paper titled 'Can Blockchain Technology Help Promote New Tourism Destinations? The Example of Medical Tourism in Moldova' (Pilkington, 2017) which later matured into a *Journal of British Blockchain Association* publication (Pilkington, 2021). A survey by Rejeb et al. (2019) evidences the benefit of blockchain technology for medical tourism and lays the ground for future research. Tyan et al. (2021) have pursued and recontextualized the research agenda through the lens of the COVID-19 pandemic. Parekh et al. (2021) emphasize the disintermediation potential of blockchain technology for medical tourism. Blockchain can enable disintermediation, medical check-up, and intervention in the pre-procedure medical tourism stage. Medical tourism requires an intermediation layer between medical service providers and tourists (Connell, 2006). The medical tourism facilitators help assess the quality of the medical tourism destination and services offered; they

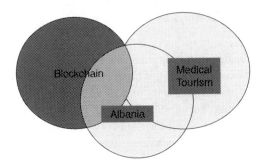

FIGURE 7.1 The intersection between three subsets.

answer queries and arrange itineraries for the medical tourists (Rejeb et al., 2019). Blockchain technology gives rise to a trustless world of medical tourism facilitators or effectively removes them by building trust, ensuring secure information exchange, reducing costs, and enabling transparency (Pilkington, 2016). In other words, blockchain technology can disintermediate the market and allow medical tourists to communicate with medical service providers directly. Blockchain technology ensures the data's origin, quality, and transparency through the interplay of electronic health records (Pilkington, 2022, p. 7), so that the medical service providers' qualifications and certifications are ensured and the equality of treatment costs for all patients is ensured. This is especially relevant for Albania, a relatively unknown and under-researched country (KAMI, 2022). Çapar (2021) and Pilkington (2022) argue that cryptocurrency transactions, in particular, and DLT, in general, are beneficial to decentralize medical tourism solutions by ensuring secure payments, easy use, rapid processing, reduced waiting times, and facilitating electronic health record management in the post-procedure phase, including monitoring for a complication, physical therapy, progress check, follow-up care, medicine instruction, clearance and return home, and follow-up care by a local healthcare provider (Ryan et al., 2021, p. 7). Smart devices and smart contracts are operated through blockchain technology with a range of healthcare applications such as temperature loggers during the shipment of drugs, tamper-proof certificates of medical necessity, and diagnosis-facilitating medical tools (Pilkington, 2021, p. 8). Figure 7.1 shows the intersection of the three subsets we focus on.

SWOT Analysis: Blockchain for Medical Tourism in Albania

Strengths

Albania spans over 28,748 km² in the South East Balkan region, which shares borders with Montenegro, Kosovo, North Macedonia, and Greece. The Albanian coast adjoins the Adriatic and Ionian Seas. Tirana is the country's financial capital,

TABLE 7.1 Top-rated hospitals and clinics in Tirana

Number	Rating	# of reviews	Clinic names
1	5	3,707	Klinika KEIT, Tirana – Albania
2	5	515	Dentisti in Albania – EndoDental
3	5	266	Kirurgjia Estetike Italiane Tirane – DaVINCI
4	5	252	Elite Dental
5	5	251	Dental Clinic KissDent
6	5	202	Alba Clinica – Dentisti in Albania
7	5	165	Klinika OrthoLUX – Digital Orthodontic Clinic
8	5	161	Klinike Dentare Emerald Dental
9	5	120	Dental ART Studio Dr. Erlira Dauti
10	5	81	Dental Tirana.al
11	5	75	Dentisti in Albania – City Dental Clinic CDC
12	5	72	Klinika dentare Lako
13	5	55	Microblading by Anxhela – Aesthetic Clinic
14	5	45	Tirana Dental Wellness
15	5	45	DR SKANA CLINIC Dr. Almir Skana
16	5	45	Klinika Dentare Dr. Erta Xhanari
17	5	41	Dentisti in Albania – Turismo Dentale – Clinica Dentale Kiss Dent
18	5	40	Chirurgia Estetica in Albania – Dermolife
19	5	37	Lolita Estetike
20	5	34	Travel and Smile

Source: https://www.top-rated.online/countries/Albania/cities/Tirana/Hospitals+%26+Clinics/top-rated.

but Vlore and Durres also attract substantial foreign direct investment. Albania is a member of WTO and NATO and a candidate for accession to the EU. Formerly the first atheist state under the Hoxha dictatorship during the Cold War (Fevziu, 2016), modern Albania is characterized by religious tolerance and diversity (Melady, 2013), and has signed free trade agreements with the EU, CEFTA, and EFTA countries, and Turkey (US Department of State, 2022). As stated in Part I, Albania prides itself on some stunning coastlines, soaring mountain peaks, tranquil lakes, UNESCO World Heritage Ottoman architecture, ancient Greek and Roman ruins, locally sourced and delicious Mediterranean cuisine, and well-preserved traditions (Responsible Travel, 2022).

A booming medical area for foreigners in Albania is hair transplants. For instance, using the follicular unit transplant (FUT) and follicular unit extraction (FUE) techniques under local anesthesia, a medical service provider in Tirana called Hair Sure – Hair Transplant Centre (2022) guarantees a success rate between 86% and 95%. Albanian specialists have often acquired skills in Germany, Italy, or Turkey and commonly speak several languages. Another promising area is plastic (more precisely cosmetic) surgery, which consists of reconstructing body parts (nose, ears, breasts, etc.). There is also an increasingly popular technique of face remodeling through Botox injections. In this respect, Dr. Kostandin Balloma (RTV Klan, 2019) is a medical service pioneer in Albania for foreigners.

Weaknesses

Kesar and Rimac (2011) and Kiss (2015) explain that the Albanian healthcare sector suffers from several weaknesses, such as poor infrastructure and insufficient service quality, education levels, training, and skills. The Balkan region suffers from a reputational deficit (Lubowiecki-Vikuk & Kurkowiak, 2017, p. 286). Further, there is a lack of cooperation between the Albanian healthcare and tourism sectors (ibid.).

The COVID-19 pandemic has deeply affected Albanian tourism as the number of foreign tourists in 2020 (about 2.4 million) was down from nearly 4 million in 2019 (6.1 million) (INSTAT, 2020).

Another issue plaguing Albania is the brain drain and massive emigration, a phenomenon not alien to medical professionals (ibid.). Among the noteworthy priorities for the Albanian tourism sector, Marku (2014, p. 65) mentions road safety, disease prevention awareness, and food safety practices through educational campaigns in the hospitality sector and vocational schools, with an emphasis on personal hygiene, the application of best practices in the handling of meat, poultry, fish, and shellfish, as well as water temperature and cleaning techniques. There is a need for enhanced emergency medical attention and the treatment of tourists suffering from serious illnesses or personal injuries (ibid., p. 66). Among its key recommendations, the Australian government (2022) advises travelers to Albania to exercise high caution due to the strained healthcare system, to be wary of diseases such as tuberculosis, typhoid, hepatitis, brucellosis, and rabies, to drink only boiled or bottled water, and to avoid raw or undercooked food.

Despite its tremendous cultural wealth, Albania is the fourth poorest country in Europe ($5,373 GDP per capita in 2022), characterized by a rising divide between the entrepreneurial elite and the disadvantaged fringe of the population, among other things, the elderly, the rural population, the school dropouts, and the illiterates (Responsible Travel, 2022).

On top of confidentiality issues pertaining to healthcare-related data (see the next section), another DLT shortcoming is that the technology is not suited for storing voluminous amounts of (or high velocity) data because of the many processing nodes that need to verify and store the data by holding identical copies of the ledger (Esposito et al., 2018). Another significant limitation lies in the lack of standardization of blockchain architectures, also known as the interoperability problem, which is detrimental to the collaboration between healthcare professionals (Morkunas et al., 2019; Pilkington, 2022). Despite the fantastic potential of smart contracts for the healthcare industry (Pilkington, 2022), some authors note that regulatory constraints exist in several countries, with medical applications preventing the rollout of smart contracts (Morkunas et al., 2019). In these times of acute energy crisis, the problematic environmental sustainability of blockchain systems relies on Proof-of-Work consensus mechanisms (Pilkington, 2016, p. 241).

Opportunities

Lubowiecki-Vikuk and Kurkowiak (2017, p. 286) argue that the brain drain issue of medical professionals can be tackled by "adequate government support, an innovative approach to eliminating defects and the use of the opportunities and observation of contemporary trends in the market." Smith et al. (2016) believe that the medical tourism market potential is huge. Therefore, more agencies will specialize in this niche in the future, creating new bilateral trade opportunities.

Marku (2014, p. 60) puts forward a graphical representation of the Albanian tourism sector distinguishing between the core tourism product ("Discovery of Albania") and specialized ones (archeology, history, trekking, culinary, etc.), while medical tourism belongs to the latter.

> DLT company ConsenSys has partnered with World Identity Network to tackle the problem of the fight against sex trafficking in Moldova (United Nations, 2018). This technological breakthrough could be transposed to the controlled growth of the tourism industry in Albania, with an increasing (and sometimes overlooked) risk of child sexual exploitation.
>
> *(Pulaj, 2022)*

Sibora (2022, p. 62) expounds on an Albanian perspective and a rigorous economic and legal analysis, of the feasibility of a central bank digital currency (CBDC), by citing a 2020 report of the Bank of Albania, one of the central banks currently exploring this option (Beqiri, 2020; Dyson & Hodgson, 2016; ECB, 2019; Gross & Siebenbrunner, 2019). Önder and Gunter (2022, p. 7) explain that CDBCs are blockchain-powered instruments that could benefit international tourists because cashless and contactless payment systems act as tourism-enhancing incentives.

Pilkington (2022) argue that blockchain is beneficial to consolidating the rule of law in Albania which is instrumental to the EU accession process. Although not directly related to medical tourism, blockchain-based voting solutions could help strengthen the democratic process and restore trust in politics by fighting corruption practices. Pilkington et al. (2022) remind us that Albania was one of the first European nations to adopt a cryptocurrency regulatory framework to protect users. The DLT Albanian ecosystem is nascent yet attracting cross-border investment (ibid.).

One issue with blockchain for medical tourism is the tension between the immutability property, and the need for patients to be able to manage (and sometimes delete) healthcare data under privacy laws. Pilkington (2021) explains that the IoT and pairing private and public cryptographic keys could constitute a viable solution to this problem toward a genuine patient-centric approach. Further to the complex problem of voluminous healthcare data reviewed above, Pilkington (2022) argues in favor of data lakes, an off-chain data containment system.

Let us mention the inner state festival, a unique well-being festival in Albania "where wellness, music, talks, food, and drink all play together".[2] The organizers promise mind-settling and body-bending practices such as yoga, meditation, breathwork, calisthenics, lucid dreaming, Qi Gong, running, swimming, and fitness.

The digitization of the medical tourism industry was assuredly accelerated by the COVID-19 pandemic with telemedicine, video-streaming, and video-conferencing tools (Tyan et al., 2021, 9). The pandemic has also reinforced the need for high-quality international accreditation of healthcare service providers (ibid.). In this respect, blockchain can authenticate medical certificates (such as PCR test results) at both ends of the issuer/recipient spectrum, detect fake ones, and eliminate fraud and manipulation. Blockchain can manage the travel government's documents, including at the issuance stage (ibid.).

Threats

Litter fills Albania's sea, rivers, and streets; there is generally a lack of waste disposal and recycling facilities and education in communities and schools to stop people from discarding waste inappropriately. Local municipalities dump trash freely; residents in Durres see their rubbish dumped in surrounding fields. The problem is harmful to the environment, the rivers, and the beaches that the former flow through, which become clogged. It is hazardous to people and tourism.

Rising geopolitical risk in Albania has been foreseen by Bieber et al. (2017). Further,

> Twenty-plus years after the wars that followed Yugoslavia's collapse, Western state-building efforts and the prospect of EU membership have failed to deliver hoped-for reforms in Western Balkan states or to resolve the region's lingering disputes. Russia's war in Ukraine has energized accession proponents, but EU enlargement remains a long-term project.
>
> *(International Crisis Group, 2022)*

One, therefore, needs to monitor these developments in light of the sustainability of medical tourism in Albania.

A Questionnaire-Based Empirical Study

We conducted by email a questionnaire-based survey on the potential of DLT for tourism in Albania by identifying and distinguishing between two population subsets. First, we targeted the medical profession (doctors in various specializations and medical students from reputed Albanian higher education institutions:[3] 70 respondents). Second, we focused on Albania's non-medical yet highly educated population (business and economics students from one of the leading higher education institutions, namely Epoka University, structured on the private US college model:[4] 30 respondents). One hundred and thirty questionnaires were sent out to the two sample subsets, and 100 responses were received, which amounts to a response rate of 77%. We opted for eight multiple-choice-closed-ended questions and one open-ended question, thereby allowing us to gather statistical data that were clear and easy to analyze. The results are presented hereafter in the form of pie charts.

Question 1
"How would you describe your knowledge of DLT?"
SUBSET 1

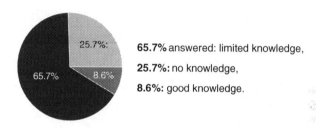

65.7% answered: limited knowledge,

25.7%: no knowledge,

8.6%: good knowledge.

FIGURE 7.2   Subset 1.

SUBSET 2

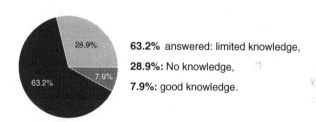

63.2% answered: limited knowledge,

28.9%: No knowledge,

7.9%: good knowledge.

FIGURE 7.3   Subset 2.

Interpretation: although Albania was one of the first countries in Europe to implement a legislative framework for cryptocurrencies (Pilkington et al., 2022), there has been little media coverage to provide the local population with relevant information on DLT. There was no significant difference between the answers of the two subsets.

Question 2
"What relationship does your business have with the tourism sector?"

SUBSET 1

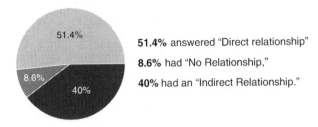

51.4% answered "Direct relationship"
8.6% had "No Relationship,"
40% had an "Indirect Relationship."

FIGURE 7.4   Subset 1.

SUBSET 2

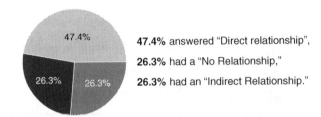

47.4% answered "Direct relationship",
26.3% had a "No Relationship,"
26.3% had an "Indirect Relationship."

FIGURE 7.5   Subset 2.

Interpretation: the first subset pertains to the healthcare sector, whereas individuals from the second subset provided answers based on their family enterprises: shops, restaurants, travel agencies, rental companies, etc. We noted that most of them are strongly connected to the tourism industry. Interestingly, respondents from the healthcare subset had a much more robust [direct + indirect relationship] total versus the other subset (91.4% versus 73.7%). The direct or indirect nature of the relationship with tourism is a purely subjective attribute of the collected data. There might exist intra-subset differences that went unnoticed by us in the first subset; while medical students and young healthcare professionals may have grown accustomed to the idea of medical tourism in Albania, older doctors more familiar with the closedness of the Communist era (Mitre, 2018) might display more psychological resistance to these new trends, thereby reinforcing the subjectivity dimension at the heart of the data.

This system allowed him [former dictator Enver Hoxha (1908–1985)] to penetrate the homes and minds of Albanians. His propaganda was based on the paranoid delusion that foreign countries plan to attack Albania. This further substantiated the need to eradicate any foreign-induced anti-Communist thoughts harbored by any citizens.

Question 3
"How can DLT enhance your business model?"

SUBSET 1

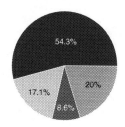

8.6% answered, "By increasing transparency,"

17.5% said, "With the increase of trust between market participants,"

20% stated, "By automating processes",

54.1% agreed with all options.

FIGURE 7.6   Subset 1.

SUBSET 2

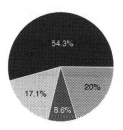

8.6% answered, "By increasing transparency,"

17.5% said, "With the increase of trust between market participants,"

20% stated, "By automating processes",

54.1% agreed with all options.

FIGURE 7.7   Subset 2.

Interpretation: we observed no significant difference between the two subsets, maybe a slightly more pronounced emphasis on transparency offered by DLT for the healthcare subset.

Question 4
"Does your organization have a DLT budget?"

SUBSET 1

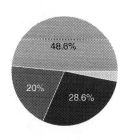

48.6% Did not have a budget but were optimistic that there would be one in the future,

28.6% Did not have a budget,

21.4% did not know,

1.4% presently had a budget.

FIGURE 7.8   Subset 1.

SUBSET 2

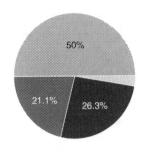

50% Did not have a budget but were optimistic that there would be one in the future,

27.2% Did not have a budget,

21.4% did not know,

1.4% <u>presently</u> had a budget.

FIGURE 7.9   Subset 2.

Interpretation: there exists no significant difference between the two subsets. Only the second subset displays more DLT awareness than the first, hinting at the need for a massive educational effort for DLT in the healthcare sector.

Question 5 (open-ended question)
"How will DLT affect existing and future business, Albanian intermediation models?"

For the first subset, the answers ranged from agreeing that it would have a positive financial impact to being unable to provide a straightforward answer owing to a lack of information about the technology. One common denominator was that DLT should be part of the future of business models. The most common (and unsurprisingly more precise) answers for the second (more blockchain literate) subset were cost reduction and facilitating digital transactions while effectively securing data integrity.

Question 6
"Do you think this technology has potential for medical tourism in Albania?"

SUBSET 1

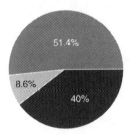

51.4% stated that they needed more information on the matter,

40% agreed that it has potential,

8.6% said no.

FIGURE 7.10   Subset 1.

SUBSET 2

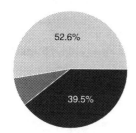

52.6% agreed that it has potential,

39.5% stated that they needed more information on the matter,

6.9% said no

FIGURE 7.11   Subset 2.

Interpretation: half of the respondents in both subsets recognized the transformative potential of DLT. The percentage of respondents who needed more information was higher among the healthcare professionals than the elite student population, hinting at better DLT knowledge of the former than the latter. A marginal proportion in both subsets saw no potential for DLT in their respective industry.

Question 7
"Would blockchain tokens be accepted by those interested in the Albanian tourism sector and would favor the development of the tourism sector?"

SUBSET 1

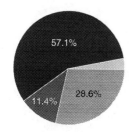

57.2% did not know what tokens are,

28.6% agreed that the tokens would be accepted with an effective promotional strategy,

11.4% thought they would neither be accepted nor favor the tourism development,

2.8% needed more information.

FIGURE 7.12   Subset 1.

SUBSET 2

60.5% agreed that the tokens would be accepted with an effective promotional strategy,

26.3% thought they would neither be accepted nor favor the development of the tourism sector,

10.5% needed more information,

12.7 % did not know what tokens were.

FIGURE 7.13   Subset 2.

Interpretation: this is an eye-opening question as DLT knowledge prerequisites were high. Unsurprisingly, lack of knowledge and skepticism prevail among the answers in the first subset, although a staggering 28.6% of all respondents did see the potential for blockchain-based tokens. For a country like Albania, the significance of this figure should not be understated. Unsurprisingly, blockchain knowledge and optimism are much higher for the second subset, denoting a positive correlation between the former and the latter. This is a step that should certainly not be overlooked by decision-makers to favor technology adoption.

Question 8
SUBSET 1

"What are the areas in which DLT would be most effective and useful in Albania?"

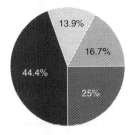

44.4% stated that the technology would be most useful in the Finance sector

25% mentioned Organization Management,

16.7% stated Tourism,

13.9% the healthcare sector.

FIGURE 7.14   Subset 1.

SUBSET 2

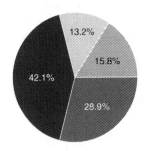

42.1% stated that the technology would be most helpful in the Finance sector,

28.9% mentioned Organization Management,

15.8% stated Tourism,

13.2% of the healthcare sector.

FIGURE 7.15   Subset 2.

Interpretation: there was no significant difference between the two subsets except the prevailing belief that the future of DLT will pertain to financial use cases with similar percentages of confidence in the healthcare and tourism industries.

Question 9

SUBSET 1
"What are the main obstacles to DLT adoption in Albania?"

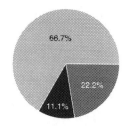

66.7% stated that the most common obstacle is the lack of information about the technology,

22.2% mentioned the cost of technology implementation,

11.1% of the increase in criminal activities.

FIGURE 7.16   Subset 1.

SUBSET 2

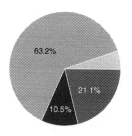

63.2% stated that the most common obstacle is the lack of information on the technology,

21.1% stated the cost of technology implementation,

10.5% answered "energy consumption",

4.2% increase in criminal activities.

FIGURE 7.17   Subset 2.

Interpretation: regrettably, a prevailing image of Albania in the world is associated with organized crime (Arsovska, 2015). This enduring stereotype is slightly stronger in Subset 1 than in Subset 2 (11.1% versus 4.2%). The persistent belief that cryptocurrencies are the vehicle for criminal activity (Kethineni & Cao, 2020) might impede broader DLT adoption in Albania and beyond.

After reviewing both subsets, we observe striking similarity patterns. The second one, composed of non-medical students in an elite university of the country, had a better grasp of the technology owing to prior DLT-related learning, exposure, and awareness. Nonetheless, there still exists a significant lack of information on the matter across both groups of respondents, particularly among the first one composed of healthcare professionals and medical students, which makes the path for DLT adoption longer as more steps need to be taken by individuals to satisfactorily comprehend the technology and learn how to implement it accordingly.

Conclusion

Although this is not always well known, Albania, a small country in the Western Balkans, has become a rising post-pandemic travel destination, offering high-quality cosmetic and medical treatments provided by internationally trained healthcare providers. Today, there exists a strong global demand for high-quality healthcare facilities backed by innovative technology. Pilkington (2021, p. 8) explains that "in medical tourism, lower medical costs, international accreditations, competent and multilingual doctors are the building blocks of enhanced attractiveness." In this chapter, we have put forward a primer on DLT and medical tourism and proposed a SWOT analysis of DLT for medical tourism in Albania. A questionnaire-based survey sector has provided much-needed empirical support to our findings. DLT improves the ability of healthcare professionals and organizations to deliver patient care in high-quality facilities, which comes together with a forecasted increase in medical tourism. Yet, lack of knowledge appears to be the most significant barrier to attaining these aims, as DLT receives little media coverage. Albanians may have heard about DLT, but many still regard it as distant and unapproachable, while stereotypes related to the illicit financing of criminal activities are not uncommon. If the promising Albanian ecosystem can overcome these cognitive barriers, the country may progress from studying and comprehending DLT to the adoption stage with concrete integration into business models. Albania would greatly benefit from DLT adoption by informing its population and building relationships with the relevant stakeholders. If the necessary steps are taken incrementally, positive changes could be observed in the realms of the economy as well as broader aspects of life.

Notes

1 https://web.archive.org/web/20050312204307/http:/www.wcb2con.com/web2con/.
2 https://innerstatefestival.com/.
3 "Our Lady of Good Counsel" University, "University of Aldent" and the Tirana Public University of Medical Sciences.
4 https://www.epoka.edu.al/.

References

Amadeus IT Group (2017). "Blockchain for travel". Retrieved from: https://www.youtube.com/watch?v=YpS0zoJ9wCU.
Arsovska, J. (2015). *Decoding Albanian organized crime: Culture, politics, and globalization*. University of California Press.
Australian Government (2022). Retrieved from: https://www.smartraveller.gov.au/destinations/europe/albania.
Beladi, H., Chao, C. C., Ee, M. S., & Hollas, D. (2015). Medical tourism and health worker migration in developing countries. *Economic Modelling, 46*, 391–396.
Belegu, A. (2021). *Albania, the Future Destination of Medical Tourism in the Balkan Region* (Doctoral dissertation, RIT Croatia).
Beqiri, G. (2020). Digital Renminbi – A technical inevitability, Bankieri No. 37, October 2020, Publication of Albanian Association of Banks, 35–37.
Bieber, F., Taleski, D., & Dimitrov, N. (2017). The avoidable return of geopolitics in the Balkans, 10 May. https://www.atlanticcouncil.org/blogs/new-atlanticist/the-avoidable-return-of-geopolitics-in-the-balkans/.
Çapar, H. (2021). Using cryptocurrencies and transactions in medical tourism. *Journal of Economic and Administrative Sciences, 37*(4), 677–693.
Connell, J. (2006). Medical tourism: Sea, sun, sand, and. surgery. *Tourism Management, 27*, 1093–1100.

Connell, J. (2013). Contemporary medical tourism: Conceptualisation, culture and commodification. *Tourism Management, 34,* 1–13.

Coleman, L. (2017). Ethereum-based Swiss blockchain startup readies tech for the food supply chain, 26 April. Retrieved from: https://www.cryptocoinsnews.com/ethereumfoodblockchainxyz-supply-chain/.

Deloitte Center for Health Solutions (2017). Medical tourism consumers in search of value. Retrieved from: http://www.deloitte.com/assets/Dcom-UnitedStates/Local%20Assets/Documents/us_chs_MedicalTourismStudy(3).pdf.

Dogru, T., Mody, M., & Leonardi, C. (2018). *Blockchain technology & its implications for the hospitality industry.* Bostom, MA: Boston University, 1–12.

Dyson, B., & Hodgson, G. (2016). Digital cash: Why central banks should start issuing electronic money. Retrieved from: https://positivemoney.

Esposito, C., De Santis, A., Tortora, G., Chang, H., & Choo, K.-K.R. (2018). Blockchain: A panacea for healthcare cloud-based data security and privacy? *IEEE Cloud Computing, 5,* 31–37.

European Central Bank (ECB) (2019). Exploring anonymity in central bank digital currencies. Focus, Issue 4. Frankfurt am Main.

Fetscherin, M., & Stephano, R. M. (2016). The medical tourism index: Scale development and validation. *Tourism Management, 52,* 539–556. https://doi.org/10.1016/j.tourman.2015.08.010.

Fevziu, B. (2016). *Enver Hoxha: The iron fist of Albania.* I.B. Tauris.

Finyear (2016). Buuyers: la blockchain garantit la fiabilité des avis clients, 21 July 2016. Available: http://www.finyear.com/Buuyers-la-blockchain.

Gross, M. M., & Siebenbrunner, C. (2019). *Money creation in fiat and digital currency systems.* International Monetary Fund.

Hair Sure – Hair Transplant Centre (2022). https://www.hairsure.in.

Horowitz, M. D., Rosensweig, J. A., & Jones, C. A. (2007). Medical tourism: Globalization of the healthcare marketplace. *Medscape General Medicine, 9*(4), 33.

Iansiti, M., & Lakhani, K. R. (2017). The truth about blockchain. *Harvard Business Review, 95*(1), 118–127.

International Crisis Group (2022). Managing the risks of instability in the western Balkans. Retrieved from: https://www.crisisgroup.org/europe-central-asia/balkans/managing-risks-instability-western-balkans.

Institute of Statistics INSTAT (2020). Popullsia e Shqipërisë. Accessed on: October 14, 2022. [Online]. http://www.instat.gov.al/media/6849/popullsia_me-_1_janar_2020.pdf.

International Air Transport Association (IATA) (2018). Blockchain in aviation – White paper. Montréal.

Iordache, C., Ciochină, I., & Roxana, P. (2013). Medical tourism–between the content and socio-economic development goals. Development strategies. *Romanian Journal of Marketing, 1,* 31–42.

Işık, C., Aydın, E., Dogru, T., Rehman, A., Sirakaya-Turk, E., & Karagöz, D. (2022). Innovation research in tourism and hospitality field: a bibliometric and visualization analysis. *Sustainability, 14*(13), 7889.

Kami (2022). Impressions from visiting Albania, 9 October. https://www.mywanderlust.pl/visiting-albania-impressions/.

Kesar, O., & Rimac, K. (2011). Medical tourism development in Croatia. *Zagreb International Review of Economics & Business, 14*(2), 107–134.

Kethineni, S., & Cao, Y. (2020). The rise in popularity of cryptocurrency and associated criminal activity. *International Criminal Justice Review, 30*(3), 325–344.

Kiss, K. (2015). The challenges of developing health tourism in the Balkans. *Tourism, 63,* 97–110.

Lubowiecki-Vikuk, A., & Dryglas, D. (2019). Medical tourism services and medical tourism destinations in central and eastern Europe-the opinion of Britons and Germans. *Economic research-Ekonomska istraživanja, 32*(1), 1256–1274.

Lubowiecki-Vikuk, A., & Kurkowiak, J. (2017). Medical tourism potential of central and eastern Europe: Attempt at classification. *CBU International Conference Proceedings, 5,* 286–293.

Lunt, N., Smith, R., Exworthy, M., Green, S. T., Horsfall, D., & Mannion, R. (2011). Medical Tourism: Treatments, markets and health system implications: A scoping review. Organisation for Economic Cooperation and Development. https://www.oecd. org/els/health-systems/48723982.pdf.

Marinau, C., Csosz, I., Martin, S. C., & Ciolac, R. (2009). European experience in the field of health tourism. Overview of the countries of western Europe, central and eastern Europe. *Agricultural Management/Lucrari Stiintifice Seria I, Management Agricol, 11*(4).

Marku, A. (2014). Tourism strategy of Albania. *European Scientific Journal, ESJ, 10*(7).

Melady, T. P. (2013). Albania: A nation of unique inter-religious tolerance and steadfast aspirations for EU integration. *Academicus International Scientific Journal, 4*(07), 12–17.

Menkshi, E., Qirici, E., & Shehu, D. (2019). Thermal springs of Benja-Albania, possibilities for tourism develeopment. *European Journal of Social Sciences, 58*(1), 23–31.

Microsoft (2016). Webjet and Microsoft build first-of-akind travel industry blockchain solution, November 8. https://news.microsoft.com/en-au/2016/11/08/webjet-and-microsoft-buildfirst-of-a-kind-travel-industry-blockchainsolution/#_ftn1.

Microsoft (2018). Webjet uses blockchain to simplify transaction disputes in the travel industry, 30 March. Available: https://customers.microsoft. com/fr-fr/story/webjet.

Ministry of Tourism, Culture, Youth and Sport of Albania (2005). Toward a strategy for culture tourism and ecotourism development. Ministry of Tourism, Culture, Youth and Sport of Albania.

Mitre, M. (2018). Healthcare (or lack thereof) in communist Albania, March 9. https://www.clinicalcorrelations.org/2018/03/09/healthcare-or-lack-thereof-in-communist-albania/.

Mofokeng, N., & Fatima, T. (2018). Future tourism trends: Utilizing non-fungible tokens to aid wildlife conservation. *African Journal of Hospitality, Tourism and Leisure, 7*(4), 1–20.

Morkunas, V. J., Paschen, J., & Boon, E. (2019). How blockchain technologies impact your business model. *Business Horizons, 62*(3), 295–306.

Nexhipi, O. (2018). Medical tourism management challenges: The Case of dental tourism in Albania. *European Journal of Interdisciplinary Studies, 4*(1), 80–86.

Noti, E. (2013). Web 2.0 and its influence in the tourism sector. *European Scientific Journal, 9*(20), 115–123.

Önder, I., & Gunter, U. (2022). Blockchain: Is it the future for the tourism and hospitality industry? *Tourism Economics, 28*(2), 291–299.

Önder, I., & Treiblmaier, H. (2018). Blockchain and tourism: Three research propositions. *Annals of Tourism Research, 72*(C), 180–182.

Ozdemir, A. I., Ar, I. M., & Erol, I. (2020). Assessment of blockchain applications in travel and tourism industry. *Quality & Quantity, 54,* 1549–1563.

Parekh, J., Jaffer, A., Bhanushali, U., & Shukla, S. (2021). Disintermediation in medical tourism through blockchain technology: An analysis using value-focused thinking approach. *Information Technology & Tourism*, *23*(1), 69–96.

Patrício, R., Moreira A. C., & Zurlo F (2018). Gamification approaches to the early stage of innovation. *Creativity & Innovation Management*, *27*(4), 499–511. https://doi.org/10.1111/caim.12284.

Pilkington, M. (2016). Blockchain technology: Principles and applications. In Xavier Olleros, F., & Zhegu, M. (eds.), *Research handbook on digital transformations*. Edward Elgar Publishing, 225–251.

Pilkington, M. (2017). Can blockchain technology help promote new tourism destinations? The example of medical tourism in Moldova, 11 June. Retrtieved from: https://ssrn.com/abstract=2984479.

Pilkington, M. (2021). The relation between tokens and blockchain networks: The case of medical tourism in the Republic of Moldova. *Journal of British Blockchain Association*, *4*(1). https://doi.org/10.31585/jbba-4-1-(2)2021.

Pilkington, M. (2022). Can blockchain improve healthcare management? *Technology Innovation Management Review*, *12*(1/2).

Pilkington, M., Crudu, R., & Grant, L. G. (2017). Blockchain and bitcoin as a way to lift a country out of poverty-tourism 2.0 and e-governance in the Republic of Moldova. *International Journal of Internet Technology and Secured Transactions*, *7*(2), 115–143.

Pulaj, A. (2022). Albania's tourism industry is on the rise, increasing risk of child sexual exploitation, warns new report, Global Voices, 16 October. Retrieved from: https://globalvoices.org/2022/10/16/albanias-tourism-industry-is-on-the-rise-increasing-risk-of-child-sexual-exploitation-warns-new-report.

Quintela, J., Costa, C., & Correia, A. G. (2016). Health, wellness and medical tourism: A conceptual approach, Enlightening Tourism. *A Pathmaking Journal*, *6*(1), 1–18.

Rejeb, A., Keogh, J.G., & Treiblmaier, H. (2019). The impact of blockchain on medical tourism. In *Proceedings of the WeB 2019 workshop on e-business*, Munich, Germany, 14 December.

Responsible Travel (2022). https://www.responsibletravel.com/holidays/albania/travel-guide/responsible-tourism-in-albania.

Rizzo P. (2017). An Asia-Pacific blockchain consortium is forming around food supply chain. CoinDesk, May 22. Retrieved from: http://www.coindesk.com/pwcteams-up-with-alibaba-for-food-supply-blockchaintest.

Romaniuk, P., & Szromek, A. R. (2016). The evolution of the health system outcomes in Central and Eastern Europe and their association with social, economic and political factors: An analysis of 25 years of transition. *BMC Health Services Research*, *16*, 1–12.

RTV Klan (2019). Histori shqiptare nga Alma Çupi – Kostandin Balloma, kirurgu qe sjell risi ne ORL! (09 shkurt 2019). Retrieved from: https://www.youtube.com/watch?v=6mYt8ixCzp4.

Sibora, S. (2022). Central Bank digital currencies: To issue, or not to issue, that is the question. Legal and economic implications in the EU and, the Albanian perspective. *European Journal of Accounting, Auditing and Finance Research*, *10*(8), 56–77.

Smith, R., Álvarez, M. M., & Chanda, R. (2011). Medical tourism: A review of the literature and analysis of a role for bi-lateral trade. *Health Policy*, *103*(2–3), 276–282.

Smith, M., Puczkó, L., Michalkó, G., Kiss, K., & Sziva, I. (2016). Balkan wellbeing and health tourism study. Final Report. MetropolitanUniversity, Budapest. http://infota.org/wpcontent/uploads/2016/03/BalkanWellbeingFINALREPORT.

Sun, S., Zhong, L., Law, R., Li, X., Deng, B., & Yang, L. (2022). Health tourism evolution: A review based on bibliometric analysis and the China National Knowledge Infrastructure Database. *Sustainability*, *14*, 10435. https://doi.org/10.3390/su141610435.

Swacha, J. (2019). Architecture of a dispersed gamification system for tourist tractions. *Information*, *10*(1), 33.

Tamminen, T. (2004). Cross-border cooperation in the southern Balkans: Local, national, or European identity politics? *Southeast European and Black Sea Studies*, *4*(3), 399–418. https://doi.org/10.1080/1468385042000281620.

Turizmi në Shifra (2019). Instat. Retrieved from: http://www.instat.gov.al/al/publikime/librat/2021/turizmi-n%C3%AB-shifra-2019.

Tyan, I., Guevara-Plaza, A., & Yagüe, M. I. (2021). The benefits of blockchain technology for medical tourism. *Sustainability*, *13*(22), 12448.

United Nations (2018). ConsenSys wins #Blockchain4Humanity challenge for designing blockchain-based identification system to help end child trafficking in Republic of Moldova, Presss Release, 15 March. Retrieved from: https://www.un.org/press/en/2018/pi2224.doc.htm.

US Department of State (2022). 2022 investment climate statements: Albania. Retrieved from: https://www.state.gov/reports/2022-investment-climate-statements/albania/.

Weis, J. L., Sirard, R. B., & Palmieri, P. A. (2017). Medical tourism: The role of the primary care provider. *BJGP Open*, *1*(2), 1–4.

Wright, A., & De Filippi, P. (2015). *Decentralized blockchain technology and the rise of lex cryptographia*. Available at SSRN 2580664.

Ylli, L. (2016). Developing Albanian tourism. *Academic Journal of Interdisciplinary Studies*, *5*(3 S1), 279–279.

8

ENHANCING SUSTAINABLE TOURISM THROUGH BLOCKCHAIN-BASED TOKENIZATION

A Novel Approach for Revenue Generation

Irem Onder

Introduction

Tourism and hospitality is one of several volatile industries that have been especially impacted by the COVID-19 pandemic (Farzanegan et al., 2021). To prevent the spread of the virus, governments all around the world have mandated lockdowns, travel bans, border closings, and compulsory quarantines for travelers. According to the WTTC and Oxford Economics (2020), in 2020, the industry lost almost US$4.7 trillion due to the pandemic. Moreover, the industry's contribution to the global GDP decreased to 5.5% in 2020, compared to 10.4% in 2019. In some cases, governments provided financial aid to the industry, but, considering its size, these subsidies cannot cover all losses. As of early 2022, the pandemic is still ongoing with limited or declining government support, thus making it prudent that managers and destinations start thinking about the future and explore new business opportunities independent of physical travel. To sustain and grow cash flow, the industry must learn to quickly adapt to disruptions while maintaining operations and safeguarding its financial viability through creative business models. As the tourism and hospitality industry faces multiple transitional and transformational changes, these new business models must embrace values based on the principles of efficient processes, agility, innovation, entrepreneurial drive, and financial viability.

Sustainable tourism is essential for tourism growth as a means of promoting economic development while ensuring environmental and social sustainability. As tourism continues to grow and diversify, it has become imperative to consider its impact on destination communities and ecosystems. From reducing carbon emissions to protecting fragile ecosystems and promoting cultural heritage, sustainable tourism provides a roadmap for the tourism industry to operate responsibly and mitigate its negative impacts (Xia et al., 2022).

DOI: 10.4324/9781003351917-8

Cultural heritage is an important aspect of human history, as it reflects the values, beliefs, and traditions of a community or society. Protecting and maintaining cultural attractions is important for several reasons. First, these sites serve as reminders of the rich cultural diversity that exists across the world. They help to promote cross-cultural understanding and appreciation, fostering a sense of unity and respect for different beliefs and ways of life. Second, cultural attractions often hold significant economic value, as they attract tourists from all over the world. They can boost local economies, create jobs, and promote sustainable tourism, which can have positive ripple effects on the wider community. Furthermore, cultural attractions play a vital role in preserving history and heritage. These sites also serve as important educational resources, providing opportunities for people of all ages to learn about different cultures, traditions, and ways of life (Richards, 2000).

In order to protect and maintain cultural attractions, it is important to prioritize their preservation and allocate appropriate resources toward their upkeep. Governments, non-profit organizations, and communities all have a role to play in ensuring that these sites are preserved for future generations. This may involve implementing measures to prevent damage or destruction, such as installing protective barriers or limiting access to sensitive areas. It may also involve investing in restoration and maintenance programs to ensure that these sites remain in good condition and continue to attract visitors. Technology, such as blockchain, can also help to create new ways of financial profitability to cope with the maintenance and sustainability of these attractions.

Blockchain is a foundational technology that paves the way for new economic and social systems (Iansiti & Lakhani, 2017). It has been popularized by cryptocurrencies such as Bitcoin and Ether, but recent applications have illustrated the far-reaching potentials of the technology. The above-mentioned smart contracts, in combination with tokenization, can open new income revenues for the hospitality and tourism industry. In this regard, the term "Internet of Value" refers to the "digitalization of assets such as 'intellectual and digital properties, equity and wealth,' as well as their transfer in an 'automated, secure, and convenient manner'" (Goanta, 2020, p. 142). Blockchain is a disruptive technology and is predicted to have long-term effects on organizations—hence the need to approach it strategically and embed it adequately into organizations to attain competitiveness (Rejeb et al., 2020).

In recent years, non-fungible tokens (NFTs), which are created and sold on blockchain, have gained significant attention for their potential to revolutionize various industries, including art, gaming, and sports. The unique nature of NFTs has also sparked interest in the marketing domain, as brands explore innovative ways to engage consumers and promote their products and services (Sestino et al., 2022). NFTs are digital tokens built on blockchain technology that represent ownership of a unique digital asset, such as art, music, or virtual real estate (Kramer et al., 2022). Unlike cryptocurrencies, which are fungible and have equal value, each NFT is distinct and carries its own value based on its rarity, provenance, and demand.

The tokenization of tourism assets is a logical starting point to explore its further application. Blockchain-based tokenization promises more efficient and inclusive business models through greater liquidity, transparency, and accessibility (Laurent et al., 2018). Indeed, it is possible to tokenize physical assets, allowing them to be easily transferred to another person on the blockchain (Roth et al., 2021). In this context, both fungible tokens and NFTs represent unique assets that could be of special interest to the tourism industry. The present study focuses on tokenizing tourist attractions and creating NFTs and their potential for creating alternative financing and revenue channels in the tourism industry. More specifically, we conceptualize how assets can be tokenized for sustainable financial gains in the tourism industry. The tokenization process is explained for a built heritage, including the steps needed for the tokenizing process and the gaining of revenue from these tokens. The benefits and challenges of tokenization for the tourism industry and individual travelers are outlined from the perspective of stakeholder theory.

This chapter is structured as follows. Section "Theoretical Perspective: Stakeholder Theory" presents the theoretical framework for the study: stakeholder theory, followed by literature review explaining blockchain tokenization and NFTs as well as what distinguishes them from fungible tokens. In Section "Blockchain and Tokenization," the conceptualization of NFTs for the tourism industry is explained, followed by a discussion of the specific benefits of tokenization in Section "Background on NFTs." The study concludes with managerial and theoretical implications as well as limitations and promising avenues for further research in Section "Benefits of Tokenization for Stakeholders."

Theoretical Perspective: Stakeholder Theory

Tourism attraction maintenance and sustainability can also be viewed through the lens of stakeholder theory, which recognizes that organizations have a responsibility to consider the needs and interests of all stakeholders involved in their operations, including employees, customers, suppliers, and the wider community (Friedman & Miles, 2006). From the viewpoint of stakeholders, it is vital to recognize that managers bear responsibilities beyond attending to shareholders' interests, which implies that maximizing value should not be the exclusive aim of a company (Khazaei et al., 2015). In the realm of tourism attraction preservation and sustainability, the stakeholder theory necessitates that tourism operators and managers actively engage with and harmonize the requirements of all parties involved in the development and upkeep of attractions. Such stakeholders may encompass local communities, tourists, businesses, and the natural environment.

Local communities are important stakeholders in tourism attraction maintenance and sustainability because they often have a vested interest in the protection and preservation of their cultural heritage and natural resources. To ensure that attractions are developed and managed in a way that is socially responsible, tourism operators and managers must engage with local communities to understand their needs and concerns and incorporate their feedback into decision-making processes. Tourists are another key stakeholder in tourism attraction maintenance and sustainability, as they are the primary users of the attraction. To ensure that tourists have positive experiences, tourism operators and managers must develop and maintain attractions in a way that is environmentally and socially responsible, such as by minimizing negative impacts on the environment and local communities.

Businesses and the wider community are also important stakeholders in tourism attraction maintenance and sustainability. For example, local businesses may benefit from increased tourism, but they may also be negatively impacted if tourism development is not managed responsibly. To ensure that tourism development benefits the wider community, tourism operators and managers must work collaboratively with local businesses and organizations to identify opportunities for mutual benefit and develop strategies to mitigate any negative impacts. Moreover, in sustainable tourism, there are often conflicting interests among different stakeholders, which can make it challenging to develop and manage attractions in a way that is socially, culturally, and environmentally responsible. Some of these include the following:

Local communities vs. tourists: Local communities often have a vested interest in protecting and preserving their cultural heritage and natural resources, while tourists are more interested in experiencing new cultures and activities. This can create conflict when tourism development is seen as a threat to local traditions or natural resources.

Businesses vs. the environment: Businesses involved in tourism may prioritize profit over environmental sustainability, which can lead to negative impacts on the natural environment. For example, businesses may be more likely to engage in unsustainable practices such as overdevelopment, waste generation, and excessive energy consumption if it means increased profits.

Governments vs. local communities: Governments may prioritize tourism development as a means of generating revenue and creating jobs, while local communities may be more concerned with preserving their cultural heritage and natural resources. This can create conflict when tourism development is seen as a threat to local traditions or natural resources.

Tourists vs. the environment: Tourists may prioritize their own enjoyment and comfort over environmental sustainability, which can lead to negative impacts on the natural environment. For example, tourists may be more likely to engage in unsustainable practices such as littering, damaging fragile ecosystems, or consuming resources at unsustainable levels.

Overall, the conflicting interests of different stakeholders in sustainable tourism can create significant challenges for tourism operators and managers. To address these challenges, it is important to engage with stakeholders and develop strategies that balance their needs and interests, while also ensuring that tourism development is socially, culturally, and environmentally responsible. Blockchain technology and tokenization of tourism assets can be a solution for further development of sustainable tourism. Consequently, we argue that within the realm of NFTs, it is crucial to assess how NFTs might achieve sustainable financial returns by adhering to the principles of stakeholder theory, as proposed by Freeman et al. (2007). These principles encompass consideration for stakeholders such as local communities, tourists, businesses, and the natural environment. Furthermore, Wilson et al. (2022) have encouraged research on stakeholder theory to gain deeper insights into the NFT phenomenon. In response to this call, we suggest that blockchain technology and the tokenization of tourism assets may serve as a viable solution for promoting sustainable tourism development.

Blockchain and Tokenization

Defining tokens, token types, and NFTs, a token can be defined as "a unit of value that represents an asset, specific use, or form of payment" (Treiblmaier, 2021, p. 2). The tokenization of assets refers to "the process of issuing a blockchain token that digitally represents a real tradeable asset" (Laurent et al., 2018, p. 63). Thus, any physical and digital asset can be tokenized, and anything that has uniquely identifying features can be turned into an NFT.

One of the key advantages of blockchain tokenization is the potential for increased liquidity and accessibility of assets. By representing assets as digital tokens on a blockchain, individuals and institutions can easily buy, sell, and transfer ownership of these assets in a secure and transparent manner. This can reduce transaction costs, increase market efficiency, and enable new investment opportunities for individuals who may not have had access to these assets in the past. Another potential advantage of blockchain tokenization is the ability to fractionalize assets. Traditional investments such as real estate or artwork are often prohibitively expensive for most investors, but by breaking these assets down into smaller tokens, individuals can invest in fractions of the asset, making these investments more accessible. This structure can be implemented for creating a new income stream for tourism attractions. Various token standards exist on different platforms that indicate the features of a specific token (e.g., ERC-20, ERC-721, and ERC-1155 on the Ethereum blockchain).

Treiblmaier (2021) differentiates between three types of tokens: payment, utility, and investment. The first category is primarily used for payment purposes, while utility tokens grant their holders specific rights, and investment tokens (aka security tokens) are bought to acquire a share of an asset or constitute a loan. In terms of tradability, tokens can be categorized as fungible or non-fungible. Each fungible token has an identical form and value, somewhat comparable to a banknote. In comparison, NFTs represent a unique asset. However, it is noteworthy to mention that the traceability feature of blockchain marks the differentiation

TABLE 8.1 Fungible and NFT differences

Fungible tokens *Example: Ethereum ERC-20*	NFTs *Example: Ethereum ERC-721*
Interchangeable: A token can be easily exchanged with the same type of token.	*Not interchangeable*: A NFT represents a unique asset.
Uniform: All fungible tokens of the same type are identical.	*Unique*: Each token is special.
Divisible: Tokens can be easily divided into smaller units.	*Non-divisible*: Tokens cannot be divided after the minting process.

Adapted from Mofokeng and Matima (2018).

between fungible and non-fungible hard at times. For example, while a specific Bitcoin is frequently perceived as a fungible token, it would be possible to trace back its history, and users could refuse the acceptance of coins that have previously been involved in illegal activities. Table 8.1 illustrates the difference between fungible tokens and NFTs.

NFTs have additional properties pertaining to standardization, interoperability (i.e., use within multiple ecosystems), tradability (trading outside of the originating environments), liquidity, immutability, provable scarcity, and programmability. By using smart contracts, developers can create limited numbers of items as NFTs and ensure that certain properties do not change over time via on-chain coding (Finzer, 2020).

The Ethereum blockchain is one of the most important platforms for tokenization. This platform allows the creation of tokens based on smart contracts (Weingärtner, 2019). NFTs represent examples of such smart contract-based tokens. According to Clack et al. (2017, p. 2), "a smart contract is an automatable and enforceable agreement. Automatable by computer, although some parts may require human input and control. Enforceable either by legal enforcement of rights and obligations or via tamper-proof execution of computer code." The smart contract includes the list of the addresses of the token owners and their balances. The underlying algorithm defines the values of tokens, the number of tokens created, their denominations, and the traffic of tokens (i.e., under which name and address and how the tokens have been spent). To own tokens, a user needs a digital wallet, which has a private key linked to the user's address and the contract address of the tokens on the blockchain itself.

NFTs first became popular among digital artists. By using NFTs, they can decide whether they also want to hand over the copyright of the product together with the purchase of their digital art. The terms of the sale are openly written on NFT auction markets. The system works similar to eBay: the buyer who has the highest bid at the end of the sale can purchase the item in question. Thus, the playing field for all artists becomes more equal because anyone can create NFTs. Moreover, the artist can choose not to give away the copyright when they sell a work of art, asking instead for a licensing fee each time it is used. NFTs are also popular among the digital gaming, collectibles, and digital art scenes. Decentralized naming services are another natural fit for NFTs, given their similarity to Internet domain names (albeit in a decentralized form). Recently, the Austrian postal service even offered NFTs to the purchasers of official stamps (Finzer, 2020). Moreover, tourism attractions can work with artists to create digital artwork of museum pieces as well as attractions as NFTs, then sell these on the NFT market to support the sustainability of the maintenance of these sites and create an additional revenue stream. This is also another tourism product that can be used for promotion of the tourist attraction.

Background on NFTs

NFTs are unique digital assets that employ blockchain technology. Ownership of NFTs is secured and traded through smart contracts on the global blockchain network, with all nodes verifying their authenticity (Dowling, 2022; Lee et al., 2023). NFTs have gained recognition in different industries, from marketing to finance. More recently, academia has also shown a growing interest in the study of NFTs. Scholars who have contributed to this field have mainly focused on financial topics, such as pricing patterns, risks and returns, and diversification roles of NFTs (e.g., Horky et al., 2022; Karim et al., 2022; Umar et al., 2022; Urom et al., 2022; Yousaf & Yarovaya, 2022), as well as marketing (e.g., Hofstetter et al., 2022).

While NFTs have been extensively researched in the finance literature, other areas, such as tourism, have not received the same level of attention. Even though NFTs have drawn attention from the business industries, the scholars have not paid enough attention to NFTs in tourism and hospitality yet. For example, Travala.com, an online travel agency founded in 2017, has recently launched its first collection of NFTs called Travel Tigers. The collection comprises 1,000 utility NFTs, with only 900 available for sale and the remaining 100 kept by the company for marketing and funding purposes. Travala.com is recognized for its crypto and blockchain-friendly approach, accepting more than 80 cryptocurrencies and fiat currencies for payment and utilizing its AVA token for various reward programs and discounts since its establishment (Menze, 2022). Another important example is Marriott International, which has positioned itself as a frontrunner in the implementation of innovative technologies. In the hotel industry, Marriott was the first to adopt NFT technology. The initiative began with Marriot Bonvoy partnering with digital artists Erick Nicolay, JVY, and TXREK to create artwork inspired by the Marriott marketing campaign (Bardwell, 2021).

On another side, in the existing literature, Go and Kang (2023) have paid attention to the importance of NFTs in creating a sustainable service ecosystem in the metaverse. There is a huge gap in the existing literature to investigate NFTs in the tourism and hospitality industry. To fill this gap, in this chapter, we use stakeholder theory as a framework for sustainable tourism development using blockchain and tokenization. We illustrate the tokenization of tourist attractions as cryptocurrency (fungible token) and NFTs. Furthermore, we examine the benefits and challenges of tokenization for the tourism industry and individual travelers. By shedding light on the potential of tokenization in tourism, this study provides valuable insights into this emerging area and highlights the need for further research.

Exemplary Tokenization Process of Tourism Assets

The tokenization process of tourism attractions resembles that of any other physical asset. This process and the benefits for the tourism industry are explained in the next section by using the tokenization of built heritage as an example. The sustainability of destinations and tourist attractions is one of the most important issues for tourism destinations. When it comes to building attractions such as the Eiffel Tower, maintenance and renovation are essential. Financial resources for attractions may come from a range of sources such as city municipalities and tourism ministries, which vary widely based on the respective country and its regulations. However, the maintenance and renovations of attractions are needed regardless of the financial resources available. The conservation of built cultural heritage is usually a long-term project that requires constant financial input. Given that these sites are usually those tourist attractions that lure the most visitors to destinations, their importance for the destinations is undeniable. One issue with these types of tourist attractions is deterioration due to natural, human, physical, and chemical factors (Eken et al., 2019), and weather conditions such as snow, wind, and earthquakes, as well as vandalism can exacerbate the problem of deterioration.

Traditionally, the maintenance of built heritage has been funded by local municipalities and various restoration funds and specialized organizations focused on the conservation of built heritage. For instance, Monumentenwacht (Monument Watch) is a non-profit international organization that oversees the periodic inspection, maintenance, and preventive conservation of built heritage (Wu & Van Laar, 2021). The organization was formed in 1973 in the Netherlands, then spread to other European countries such as Belgium, Germany, the UK, Denmark, Hungary, and France. It has more than 5,000 nongovernmental members (Eken et al., 2019). The like-minded International Council on Monuments and Sites (ICOMOS) is dedicated to the conservation of the world's sites and monuments (ICOMOS, 2021). In light of the difficulties of raising funding for conservation purposes, tokenization can provide an alternative way for them to finance built heritage.

Appraisal of built heritage is the first step of tokenization. According to Provins et al. (2008), heritage assets like the Eiffel Tower may be considered economic goods that contribute to human well-being. The economic value of these heritage assets is seen as proportional to the monetary value of well-being that individuals gain from them. Because conservation and restoration of built heritage are associated with positive values, the deformation of these assets has negative effects on the well-being of those who admire them. Consequently, the public is willing to pay to mitigate the damage and decay of built heritage. Key methods for the appraisal of heritage assets include willingness to pay, value transfer, stated preference, and choice modeling.

After the appraisal of the tourism asset, the next step is to create the tokens, which can be both fungible and non-fungible. Let us continue with our example of the Eiffel Tower, the value of which must then be determined. Appraisal of the value of the tower can be accomplished with the help of tourism experts, who, in this hypothetical situation, determine its worth to be 435 billion euros (cf. Samuel, 2012). In case fungible tokens are chosen, this step is followed by issuing tokens equal to that value. The value of each token can be decided by the owner of the asset. By way of illustration, let us assume that each token is decided to be worth 500 euros, meaning that the owner issues 870 million fungible tokens. A buyer can purchase as many tokens as they want and resell these tokens whenever they wish.

In terms of NFTs, the owner can also decide how many will be created. If 5,000 NFTs are created in addition to the fungible tokens, and because they are

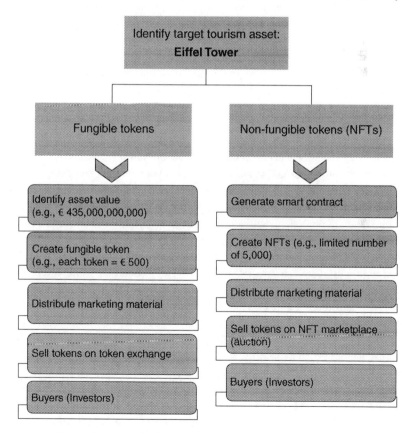

FIGURE 8.1 Exemplary tokenization process of the Eiffel Tower.

limited and unique, they can be sold on NFT marketplaces such as Mintable or Rarible. The value of each NFT is defined by the results of NFT marketplace actions. In both cases, potentially fungible and NFTs can be resold again by a buyer on the blockchain, but in the case of NFTs, additional properties and rights can be specified. For example, the owners of NFTs might be allowed to join a special club with additional incentives such as regular meetings or discounts. Figure 8.1 shows such a tokenization process of the Eiffel Tower with fungible and NFTs.

Benefits of Tokenization for Stakeholders

One advantage of tokenizing real-world assets is that these tokens are easily tradable on blockchains via secondary markets (Laurent et al., 2018). By tokenizing and selling an asset, the creator or owner receives a financial gain. The benefits for a tourism attraction that owns a tokenized asset include receiving extra financial contributions from consumers on blockchains. In addition, new work opportunities open up for artists and computer programmers who create digital assets as NFTs. Thus, in this case tokenization has benefits for the tourism industry and artists from the creation and selling of NFTs.

The appraisal of tourism assets is a huge topic on its own and includes the involvement of tourism experts and other stakeholders impacted by tourism marketing activity such as residents and shop owners in touristic areas. If the tokenized asset is an NFT, the creator of the NFT (the owner of the asset) can continue to reap monetary benefits as long as that NFT is traded on the blockchain. This is another way of getting revenues from the physical tourism asset, which can be used for maintenance and sustainability of the attractions.

Benefits for tourists or consumers of buying tokens include reselling of tokens (especially NFTs), which can be resold again at higher values. Because NFTs are scarce, their value is expected to increase over time in case they represent an appealing asset, making them a novel investment opportunity. The value of an NFT is usually determined as would be the case on an art auction circuit. Moreover, heritage assets have benefits to society. They enhance local identity and pride, lead to economic spillovers that are beneficial for local businesses, and offer educational value to the public (Cwi, 1980). Further benefits of NFTs for consumers can be designed and implemented by the creators of those NFTs. For instance, if an individual buys one of the 5,000 limited Eiffel Tower tokens in the above example, the consumer (NFT buyer) can have a JPEG of the tower created by an artist, along with other benefits such as priority access to the tower and participation in special events for the tower's NFT buyers hosted on the tower at night. Such benefits could be organized by the Eiffel Tower administration and the Paris Convention and Visitors Bureau. This system would be very similar to museum memberships, only on a digital basis. Moreover, consumers who bought NFTs can resell them for a profit, given their limited nature. Thus, buying these NFTs is like investing in real-world art pieces such as paintings by famous artists.

Another benefit for the tourism industry is that tokenized assets can create a market specifically for tourism products, including virtual tours in tokenized museums or other heritage sites. A destination can create a portfolio of tourism products such as a three-day tour of Istanbul, a visit to the Louvre, and the ability to shop for local products. For instance, Amazon already launched tourism experience products on its Amazon Explore page during the COVID-19 pandemic. Users can purchase live and interactive tours with local guides, as well as shop in local stores by paying through the Amazon website. The products are not only city tours but also culinary experiences. For instance, an individual can purchase a sushi-making class with a chef from Japan. This is a live and interactive experience as well. Technology-driven tourism experiences similar to the tokenized destinations and built heritage assets result in the co-creation of experiences.

Conclusion and Discussion

As we are shifting toward a decentralized economy, new opportunities are arising. One of these opportunities is found in tokenization based on public blockchains. The nature of tourism and hospitality assets and their product offerings make them suitable for numerous tokenization opportunities, thus creating alternative ways of generating revenues. This offers substantial implications for academics and practitioners.

Theoretical Implications

The tokenization options outlined in this conceptual chapter pose the next step in the further digitalization and transformation of the tourism and hospitality industry. While blockchain applications have already been developed to facilitate booking, payment, and supply chain processes within the industry, the tokenization of physical and virtual assets is a comparatively new and unexplored topic. In this regard, a substantial amount of rigorous research is needed to better understand how this phenomenon can potentially contribute value, how it will shape the industry, and which factors might decide its ultimate adoption. We have suggested stakeholder perspective as a potential starting point. Of course, this does not exclude other theoretical approaches, but the investigation of how tokens can provide value for tourism organizations by strengthening their internal resources, shaping their external relationships, and being accepted by customers will provide a solid starting point for scholars working in that area. While a solid amount of literature on sustainable tourism and respective theories already exists, further operationalizations and modifications are needed to account for the idiosyncrasies of tokenization. This is especially important in an area that is characterized by a plethora of different applications, each with its unique properties and features. By carefully investigating and structuring the domain, academia will be able to lay the foundation for future incremental research and create an understanding of how tokenization will impact the industry and its customers alike.

Managerial Implications

Tourism and hospitality assets consist of a wide array of cultural and heritage attractions, including cities as destinations, historical artifacts housed in museums, and the like. It is possible to represent specific resources and assets of the industry by some predetermined or assessed numbers of tokens on a public blockchain, with each token standing for a fractional value of a given attraction or artifact with its own NFT. Thus, issued blockchain-based tokens can be easily created, traded, stored, and transferred in the digital world. Through fractional ownership, tourism assets of all sizes can be made accessible on a secure online platform. They also become tradeable on secondary markets, thus allowing a broader base of investors to participate in the financial ecosystem toward the generation of new revenues. Moreover, the destination or the attraction would directly benefit from the financial gain without the need of a middleman such as a bank. Tokenized assets remove both physical barriers and infrastructural limits.

In addition to creating financial viability, the tokenization of tourism attractions via NFTs offers several advantages for sustainable tourism practices and managing attractions more efficiently. By holding tokens, travelers are no longer mere consumers but also, to some extent, owners of the asset, thus fostering a sense of shared responsibility for the product and its consumption and preservation. Sustainably managing such a product shows that both demand and supply are in the best interest of the token holder as well as the attraction manager. Through the tokenization process of the product or assets, Destination Management Organizations (DMOs) and destination managers are better positioned to sustain and increase their revenue options. Increased revenues would also allow them to manage their assets more effectively. It is well known that most visits to certain destinations and attractions are seasonal. This reality makes the amount of cash flow volatility and the maintaining of quality staff more challenging. Tokenizing tourism assets would, therefore, help alleviate the financial burdens of seasonal business.

The extent of what can be tokenized in the tourism and hospitality sector may depend on the size, type, and uniqueness of the product or assets in question. These may range from a hotel or restaurant to a world heritage site, an artifact in a museum, cities as attractions, and art. Destinations that are not easily accessible yet have unique tourism products to offer could also develop new business models designed around a digital transformation strategy whereby they can be part of the real or virtual consumption of their products. By doing so, they will be able to not only sustain their business but also create additional streams of revenue.

Limitations and Further Research

There are also challenges regarding the tokenization of tourism assets. The first is the adoption of blockchain technology by the industry. Although Bitcoin and blockchain technology have been around since 2009, research into their applications beyond cryptocurrencies is nascent and the technology is constantly evolving. Therefore, research including applied case studies would be of enormous value for the tourism industry. Another concern is fostering a sense of community via blockchains. The participants of a blockchain need to agree to be on it and still have enough technical understanding before using it. Further research on this topic will allow us to develop practical solutions that industry practitioners can also implement. To make the appraisal process easier, a database of heritage sites with corresponding evaluation studies could be created. In addition to economic value, information about visitors and non-visitors such as predicted visitor numbers and frequency of visits to the heritage site would enhance the evaluation process (Provins et al., 2008). In this regard, both academic tourism experts and industry stakeholders must weigh in.

Another concern related to blockchain technology is its high-energy consumption for certain types of public and permissionless blockchains. Climate change and sustainability are increasingly prescient concerns, and the high energy consumption of this technology is one of the reasons delaying its wider adoption. Several cryptocurrencies are based on the proof of work (PoW) mechanism, which enables reaching a majority consensus on the blockchain by using computing power. However, there are other consensus mechanisms available such as proof of stake (PoS), which is energy-efficient for large-scale systems (Sedlmeir et al., 2020). Furthermore, carbon offset can be added to the prices (like airplane tickets) of NFTs and other tokens, which would help diminish the environmental concerns. Thus, leadership in tourism technology adoption promises to be the way of the future (Spencer et al., 2012).

Technology can help alleviate the consequences of economic downturns and pandemics such as COVID-19 for the tourism industry. According to Sigala (2020), technology is the heart of the revitalizing process of tourism after COVID-19. In addition to the traditional way of doing business, the tourism industry needs to think outside of the proverbial box and understand the new technologies of blockchain and tokenization and their practical applications. The application of these technologies to the tourism industry is a viable option for sustainable financial gain as shown in this study. If the tourism industry and its related research streams are to move forward, then innovative ways of using technology in the tourism industry must be investigated. It is also essential to change our perspective regarding tourism revenues and understand that blockchain can provide this via tokenized tourism assets.

This study is the first to conceptualize the tokenization of built heritage/ tourist attractions using tokens and especially NFTs. The future of the industry stands to benefit substantially from the effective use of these new technologies. Blockchain tokens both fungible and NFTs can create a sustainable way of generating income and conserving built heritage. Future studies are needed to investigate other uses of NFTs and tokenization processes from different perspectives toward overcoming the social, economic, and environmental challenges of tourism destinations. While there are valid environmental concerns about NFTs and blockchain technology, it's important to consider some counterarguments to ensure a balanced perspective:

Adoption of more energy-efficient consensus algorithms: As the blockchain ecosystem evolves, the adoption of energy-efficient consensus algorithms like PoS and Delegated Proof of Stake (DPoS) will help reduce the environmental impact. These mechanisms require far less energy compared to the traditional PoW algorithm.

Renewable energy usage: Many blockchain networks and mining facilities are transitioning to using renewable energy sources like solar, wind, and hydroelectric power. This will help minimize their environmental footprint and contribute to a more sustainable future.

Decentralized nature of blockchain: Blockchain technology's decentralized nature can promote sustainability in other sectors, such as supply chain management, by increasing transparency and reducing the need for intermediaries. This can help cut down on emissions associated with transportation and other logistics-related activities.

NFTs as a digital alternative: NFTs provide a digital alternative to physical collectibles and art, which can help reduce the environmental impact associated with producing, storing, and transporting these items. While the minting process can be energy-intensive, the overall environmental impact of NFTs may be less than that of their physical counterparts.

Incentivizing green initiatives: Blockchain and NFTs can be used to incentivize and track green initiatives, such as carbon credits and renewable energy certificates. This can help promote sustainable practices and reduce the overall environmental impact of various industries.

Technological innovation: As with any new technology, blockchain and NFTs will continue to evolve and improve. Innovations in both hardware and software can help reduce the environmental impact of these technologies over time.

Relative energy consumption: While the energy consumption of blockchain networks and NFTs is a concern, it's essential to compare it to other industries and systems that consume energy, such as traditional financial institutions, data centers, and transportation. In some cases, blockchain technology might still be more energy-efficient than existing systems.

It's crucial to continue working on addressing the environmental concerns associated with NFTs and blockchain while also acknowledging the potential benefits and improvements these technologies can bring to various industries. Overall, blockchain tokenization has the potential to transform a wide range of industries and enable new investment opportunities for individuals and institutions. However, there are also significant challenges that need to be addressed in order to fully realize the benefits of this technology. Continued research and development will be critical in addressing these challenges and unlocking the full potential of blockchain tokenization.

References

Bardwell, J. (2021). Marriott Bonvoy logs into the metaverse with debut of travel inspired NFTs. Retrieved from: https://news.marriott.com/news/2021/12/04/marriott-bonvoy-logs-into-the-metaverse-with-debut-of-travel-inspired-nfts.

Clack, C. D., Bakshi, V. A., & Braine, L. (2017). Smart contract templates: Foundations, design landscape and research directions. *ArXiv:1608.00771.* http://arxiv.org/abs/1608.00771.

Cwi, D. (1980). Public support of the arts: Three arguments examined. *Journal of Cultural Economics, 4*(2), 39–62. https://doi.org/10.1007/BF02580849.

Dowling, M. (2022). Is non-fungible token pricing driven by cryptocurrencies? *Finance Research Letters, 44*, 102097. ISO 690

Eken, E., Taşcı, B., & Gustafsson, C. (2019). An evaluation of decision-making process on maintenance of built cultural heritage: The case of Visby, Sweden. *Cities, 94*, 24–32. https://doi.org/10.1016/j.cities.2019.05.030.

Farzanegan, M. R., Gholipour, H. F., Feizi, M., Nunkoo, R., & Andargoli, A. E. (2021). International tourism and outbreak of coronavirus (COVID-19): A cross-country analysis. *Journal of Travel Research, 60*(3), 687–692. https://doi.org/10.1177/0047287520931593.

Finzer, D. (2020). The non-fungible token bible: Everything you need to know about NFTs. *OpenSea Blog.* Retrieved from: https://opensea.io/blog/guides/non-fungible-tokens/.

Freeman, R. E., Martin, K., & Parmar, B. (2007). Stakeholder capitalism. *Journal of Business Ethics, 74*(4), 303–314.

Friedman, A. L., & Miles, S. (2006). *Stakeholders: Theory and practice.* OUP.

Go, H., & Kang, M. (2023). Metaverse tourism for sustainable tourism development: Tourism agenda 2030. *Tourism Review, 78*(2), 381–394.

Goanta, C. (2020). Selling LAND in decentraland: The regime of non-fungible tokens on the ethereum blockchain under the digital content directive. In A. Lehavi, & R. Levine-Schnur (Eds.), *Disruptive technology, legal innovation, and the future of real estate* (pp. 139–154). Springer.

Hofstetter, R., de Bellis, E., Brandes, L., Clegg, M., Lamberton, C., Reibstein, D., ... & Zhang, J. Z. (2022). Crypto-marketing: How non-fungible tokens (NFTs) challenge traditional marketing. *Marketing Letters, 33*(4), 705–711.

Horky, F., Rachel, C., & Fidrmuc, J. (2022). Price determinants of non-fungible tokens in the digital art market. *Finance Research Letters, 48*, 103007.

Iansiti, M., & Lakhani, K. R. (2017). The truth about blockchain. *Harvard Business Review, 95*(1), 118–127.

ICOMOS (2021). International Council on Monuments and Sites. Retrieved from: https://www.icomos.org/en.

Karim, S., Lucey, B. M., Naeem, M. A., & Uddin, G. S. (2022). Examining the interrelatedness of NFTs, DeFi tokens and cryptocurrencies. *Finance Research Letters, 47*, 102696.

Khazaei, A., Elliot, S., & Joppe, M. (2015). An application of stakeholder theory to advance community participation in tourism planning: The case for engaging immigrants as fringe stakeholders. *Journal of Sustainable Tourism, 23*(7), 1049–1062.

Kramer, M., Graves, S., & Phillips, D. (2022). Beginner's guide to NFTs: What are non-fungible tokens? Retrieved from: https://decrypt.co/resources/non-fungible-tokens-nfts-explained-guide-learn-blockchain.

Laurent, P., Chollet, T., Burke, M., & Seers, T. (2018). *The tokenization of assets is disrupting the financial industry. Are you ready?* (No. 19; Inside. Triannual insights from Deloitte, pp. 62–67).

Lee, C. T., Ho, T. Y., & Xie, H. H. (2023). Building brand engagement in metaverse commerce: The role of branded non-fungible toekns (BNFTs). *Electronic Commerce Research and Applications*, *58*, 101248. ISO 690.

Menze, J. (2022). Travala builds NFT-based travel rewards program. Retrieved from: https://www.phocuswire.com/travala-builds-nft-based-travel-rewards-program.

Mofokeng, M., & Matima, T. (2018). Future tourism trends: Utilizing non-fungible tokens to aid wildlife conservation. *African Journal of Hospitality, Tourism and Leisure*, *7*(4), 1–20.

Provins, A., Pearce, D., Ozdemiroglu, E., Mourato, S., & Morse-Jones, S. (2008). Valuation of the historic environment: The scope for using economic valuation evidence in the appraisal of heritage-related projects. *Progress in Planning*, *69*, 131–175. https://doi.org/10.1016/j.progress.2008.01.001.

Rejeb, A., Keogh, J. G., & Treiblmaier, H. (2020). How blockchain technology can benefit marketing: Six pending research areas. *Frontiers in Blockchain*, *3*(3), 1–12. https://doi.org/10.3389/fbloc.2020.00003.

Richards, G. (2000). Tourism and the world of culture and heritage. *Tourism Recreation Research*, *25*(1), 9–17.

Roth, J., Schär, F., & Schöpfer, A. (2021). The tokenization of assets: Using blockchains for equity crowdfunding. In K. Wendt (Ed.), *Theories of change*. Springer International Publishing. https://doi.org/10.2139/ssrn.3443382.

Samuel, H. (2012). Eiffel Tower worth £344 billion to French economy—Or six towers of London. *The Telegraph*. Retrieved from: https://www.telegraph.co.uk/news/worldnews/europe/france/9492500/Eiffel-Tower-worth-344-billion-to-French-economy-or-six-Towers-of-London.html.

Sedlmeir, J., Buhl, H. U., Fridgen, G., & Keller, R. (2020). The energy consumption of blockchain technology: Beyond myth. *Business & Information Systems Engineering*, *62*(6), 599–608. https://doi.org/10.1007/s12599-020-00656-x.

Sestino, A., Guido, G., & Peluso, A. M. (2022). A review of the marketing literature on NFTs. In Sestino, A., Guido, G., & Peluso, A.M. (Eds.), *Non-fungible tokens (NFTs) examining the impact on consumers and marketing strategies* (pp. 23–41). Cham: Palgrave Macmillan.

Sigala, M. (2020). Tourism and COVID-19: Impacts and implications for advancing and resetting industry and research. *Journal of Business Research*, *117*, 312–321. https://doi.org/10.1016/j.jbusres.2020.06.015.

Spencer, A. J., Buhalis, D., & Moital, M. (2012). A hierarchical model of technology adoption for small owner-managed travel firms: An organizational decision-making and leadership perspective. *Tourism Management*, *33*(5), 1195–1208.

Treiblmaier, H. (2021). The token economy as a key driver for tourism: Entering the next phase of blockchain research. *Annals of Tourism Research*, *91*(103177), 1–4. https://doi.org/10.1016/j.annals.2021.103177.

Umar, Z., Gubareva, M., Teplova, T., & Tran, D. K. (2022). Covid-19 impact on NFTs and major asset classes interrelations: Insights from the wavelet coherence analysis. *Finance Research Letters*, *47*, 102725.

Urom, C., Ndubuisi, G., & Guesmi, K. (2022). Dynamic dependence and predictability between volume and return of non-fungible tokens (NFTs): The roles of market factors and geopolitical risks. *Finance Research Letters*, *50*, 103188.

Weingärtner, T. (2019). *Tokenization of physical assets and the impact of IoT and AI*. Lucerne University of Applied Sciences & Arts–School for Information Technology. https://

blockchain.pwias.ubc.ca/sites/blockchain.pwias.ubc.ca/files/report-files/Weingaertner_
Tokenization_IoT_AI%20(1).pdf.

Wilson, K. B., Karg, A., & Ghaderi, H. (2022). Prospecting non-fungible tokens in the
digital economy: Stakeholders and ecosystem, risk and opportunity. *Business Horizons,
65*(5), 657–670.

WTTC & Oxford Economics. (2020). WTTC / Oxford economics 2020 travel & tourism
economic impact research. Retrieved from: https://wttc.org/Portals/0/Documents/Reports/
2020/WTTC%20Methodology%20Report%202020.pdf?ver=2021-02-25-183105-660.

Wu, M., & Van Laar, B. (2021). The Monumentenwacht model for preventive conservation
of built heritage: A case study of Monumentenwacht Vlaanderen in Belgium. *Frontiers
of Architectural Research, 10*(1), 92–107. https://doi.org/10.1016/j.foar.2020.07.007.

Xia, B., Dong, S., Li, Z., Zhao, M., Sun, D., Zhang, W., & Li, Y. (2022). Eco-efficiency and
its drivers in tourism sectors with respect to carbon emissions from the supply chain: An
integrated EEIO and DEA approach. *International Journal of Environmental Research
and Public Health, 19*(11), 6951.

Yousaf, I., & Yarovaya, L. (2022). Herding behavior in conventional cryptocurrency market,
non-fungible tokens, and DeFi assets. *Finance Research Letters, 50,* 103299.

9

APPLICATION OF BLOCKCHAIN-BASED SMART CONTRACT IN SUSTAINABLE TOURISM FINANCE

Engin Demirel

Introduction

Blockchain-based smart contracts have the technological potential to develop sustainable tourism financing by enabling transparent and efficient digital transactions. Smart contracts are self-executing digital contracts stored on the blockchain network, allowing for automated and secure transactions without intermediaries (Pradhan & Singh, 2021). Utilizing this technology makes the financial process more efficient, lowers expenses, and fosters stakeholder confidence (El Khatib et al., 2021). The use of decentralized finance (DeFi) platforms to finance sustainable tourism initiatives is one of the application examples for blockchain-based smart contracts in sustainable tourism financing. These platforms utilize smart contracts to automate funding and ensure funds are used for the intended resources.

Additionally, blockchain-based smart contracts can support carbon offset trading, enabling tourists and tourism-related enterprises to offset their carbon impact with transferable and exchangeable carbon credits. This process is carried out in a transparent and auditable manner (Kahya et al., 2021). Furthermore, combining IoT devices with smart contracts can result in more sustainable and cost-effective transactions and more efficient and secure travel payments (Ozkan et al., 2021).

The Sustainable Development Goals (SDGs) have objectives that aim to promote "decent work and economic growth," "industry, innovation, and infrastructure," "responsible consumption and production," and "inclusive and equitable society" (climate action) (Fonseca et al., 2020). Blockchain-based smart contracts can enable responsible consumption and production while encouraging economic development and innovation in the travel and tourism industry (Demirel et al., 2022). An example of the implementation of blockchain-based smart contracts in

DOI: 10.4324/9781003351917-9

sustainable tourism finance is the use of DeFi platforms to fund the financing of sustainable tourism projects. These platforms promote economic growth in the tourism sector by providing alternative sources of financing while at the same time ensuring that the funds are used for their intended purposes (Zetzsche et al., 2020).

The questions that will arise in terms of providing the necessary financing for sustainable tourism with smart contracts can be summarized as follows:

- How do blockchain-based smart contracts impact the efficiency and cost-effectiveness of sustainable tourism finance transactions?
- How does integrating sustainability data into blockchain-based smart contracts encourage businesses to adopt sustainable tourism practices?
- What are the critical success factors for adopting blockchain-based smart contracts in sustainable tourism finance, and how do they change in different contexts?
- What are the main challenges and opportunities associated with implementing blockchain-based smart contracts in sustainable tourism finance, and how can they be addressed?
- What are the implications of blockchain-based smart contracts for data privacy and security in sustainable tourism finance transactions?
- What are the policy implications of adopting blockchain-based smart contracts in sustainable tourism finance, and how can governments and stakeholders collaborate to promote usage and improve sustainability outcomes?

The application of blockchain-based smart contracts in sustainable tourism finance is an evolving new technology in meeting the growing demand for transparency, accountability, and sustainability in the tourism industry. This technology lowers transaction costs and improves payment procedures by providing a decentralized and secure platform.

The SDGs and Blockchain

The concept of sustainable development emerged in the 1980s following the publication of the Brundtland Report by the World Commission on Environment and Development (WCED) in 1987. Sustainability was outlined in the report (Brundtland, 1987) as "development that meets the needs of today without compromising the ability of future generations to meet their own needs." For this purpose, global efforts are being made to achieve sustainable development. Including environmental, economic, and social sustainability, Goodland and Daly's (1996) study proposes a framework for sustainable development (Weaver & Faulkner, 2000). The SDGs (UN DESA, 2022) are a group of 17 interrelated objectives adopted by the UN in 2015 to achieve a more sustainable and equal world by 2030 (Boluk et al., 2019; Opoku, 2016).

The SDG was established by the UN in 2015 as a global call to action to eliminate poverty, reduce environmental impact, and ensure everyone lives in peace and prosperity by 2030 (Bexell and Jönsson, 2017). The 17 SDGs address various challenges, including biodiversity preservation, clean water and sanitation, gender equality, sustainable cities, clean energy, and hunger. Governments, civil societies, corporates, and individuals from all over the globe must work together to achieve these goals in pursuing a sustainable and equitable future for everyone (Graci, 2013). The following SDGs are connected to blockchain technology applications in this context, including:

Goal 8: Decent Work and Economic Growth. It encourages entrepreneurship and employment generation while promoting wealth creation, improved levels of productivity, and technological innovation.

Goal 9: Industry, Innovation, and Infrastructure. It focuses on building resilient infrastructure, promoting sustainable industrialization, and promoting innovation.

Goal 12: Responsible Consumption and Production. It aims to ensure sustainable consumption and production models, reduce waste, and promote sustainable tourism practices.

Goal 13: Climate Action. It focuses on taking urgent action to combat climate change and its impacts, including developing and implementing strategies to reduce greenhouse gas emissions and promote climate-resilient tourism.

Goal 17: Partnerships for the Goals. The SDG aims to strengthen the implementation tools for sustainable development and revitalize the global partnership to achieve its goals, including partnerships between the public and private sectors.

The relationship between the purposes of use of smart contracts based on blockchain technologies with the determined goals is as follows:

Goal 8: Using blockchain-based smart contracts can help promote transparency and accountability in tourism finance, ensure that employees are paid fairly, and ensure that financial transactions are conducted safely and efficiently. This may result in the establishment of new employment possibilities and the encouragement of long-term economic growth. According to Rashideh's research, blockchain technology can provide safe and open transactions in travel and tourism, building more stakeholder confidence (Rashideh, 2020). Upadhyay et al.'s (2021) study indicates that employing smart contracts built on the blockchain can help cut transaction costs and increase the effectiveness of financial transactions, promoting future economic growth and development. Mishra and Kaushik (2021) indicate that blockchain technology can aid in developing a decentralized and secure financial system to encourage greater financial inclusion and economic prosperity. De Villiers et al. state that blockchain technology can improve the accountability and transparency of financial transactions. This may help to promote fair and equal treatment and secure employees' rights (De Villiers et al., 2021).

According to the United Nations World Tourism Organization, tourism significantly contributes to job creation and economic growth, especially in developing countries (UNWTO, 2021). Blockchain technology can help promote transparency, accountability, and security in the tourism industry, increase trust, and positively impact job creation and economic growth. Furthermore, blockchain-based smart contracts can offer efficient payment systems that benefit employees and businesses (Pinna & Ibba, 2019). Blockchain technology may improve financial access, a crucial component of the SDGs (Aysan et al., 2021a). Blockchain-based smart contracts can promote financial inclusion in travel and tourism by delivering more open and accessible finance options, specifically in regions with limited access to conventional funding resources (Mavilia & Pisani, 2020).

Goal 9: By allowing for secure and automated processing of monitoring tourism activities and transactions, Internet of Things (IoT) device integration with blockchain-based smart contracts can further increase the industry's efficiency and transparency. Ćirić and Ivanišević show attention in a case study to the potential of blockchain-based solutions for fostering sustainability and expansion of the tourist sector's economy (Ćirić & Ivanišević, 2018). Similarly, Yeasmin and Baig's research highlighted the significance of cutting-edge technologies like blockchain and IoT in enhancing the effectiveness and sustainability of various industries (Yeasmin & Baig, 2019). According to a study by Negi et al., combining blockchain with IoT can enable swift and safe transactions using smart contracts (Negi et al., 2021). The potential for blockchain-based smart contracts to enhance supply chain management in the sector has been highlighted by Azmat and Thanou (2023). Smart contracts enable reliable and practical payments within various supply chain participants, including travel agencies, accommodation businesses, and transportation companies (Azmat & Thanou, 2023).

Additionally, blockchain-based smart contracts can aid in the creation of new, more inclusive, and sustainable business models for the tourism sector, such as community-based tourism and eco-tourism (Madanaguli et al., 2023). Smart contracts can assist the industry in reaching SDG 9: industry, innovation, and infrastructure by encouraging more effective and environmentally friendly tourism operations (Tyan et al., 2021). Smart contracts, for instance, can enable automated payments to vendors and service providers, lowering transaction costs and reducing the need for intermediary institutions. Blockchain-based smart contracts can also support the development of decentralized tourism platforms that encourage community engagement (Nam et al., 2021).

Goal 12: Blockchain technology can facilitate monitoring waste reduction and resource efficiency initiatives throughout the tourism supply chain, enabling more effective measurement and reporting of progress toward sustainability goals (Di Vaio & Varriale, 2020). Blockchain-based smart contracts can promote sustainable behavior by providing economic rewards for suppliers and service providers who adopt sustainable practices. This could help the trend toward more responsible consumption and production in tourism (Saberi et al., 2019). Integrating blockchain-based smart contracts into tourism can contribute to SDG success by providing a more transparent and traceable system for responsible consumption and production (Parmentola et al., 2022). According to Whitaker and Pawar's study examining the potential of blockchain technology in promoting sustainable tourism practices and achieving responsible consumption (Whitaker & Pawar, 2020) and production goals, blockchain-based smart contracts can help increase the transparency and traceability of tourism products and services, leading to more responsible consumption and sustainable production (Ali et al., 2020). The potential of IoT devices of blockchain technology in promoting sustainable consumption and production through efficient supply chain management and reducing waste in the production process stands out (Ghahremani-Nahr et al., 2022). Blockchain-based applications can enable decentralized and transparent management of tourism resources, facilitate sustainable financing and investment, and increase stakeholder trust and accountability (Aghaei et al., 2021).

Goal 13: Blockchain-based smart contracts can enable the creation of decentralized transport networks and demonstrate a secure and transparent way to monitor carbon emissions from transport. This technology could also encourage using low-carbon transport options such as electric vehicles, bicycles, and public transportation. Smart contracts encourage tourism businesses to adopt sustainable practices and reduce their carbon footprint by rewarding them with tokens that can be used for eco-friendly certificates. This technology can also contribute to reducing greenhouse gas emissions from the tourism sector and help achieve the goals set out in the Paris Agreement (Kim & Huh, 2020).

Blockchain-based solutions can track changes in weather patterns and natural disasters. Blockchain can facilitate sharing of climate-related data and information among tourism stakeholders and contribute to better decision-making and more effective climate action (Sivarethinamohan & Sujatha, 2021). Similarly, Saraji and Borowczak's (2021) research demonstrates the potential of blockchain-based carbon offset mechanisms in promoting sustainable development and climate action in the tourism industry (Saraji & Borowczak, 2021). Pan et al. (2019) examined the potential of blockchain and smart contracts to promote renewable energy and reduce carbon emissions (Pan et al., 2019). According to Al Sadawi et al. (2021), blockchain technology can support climate change mitigation and SDGs by increasing transparency and reducing corruption in carbon markets (Al Sadawi et al., 2021).

Goal 17: Blockchain technology can facilitate the development of partnerships between the public and private sectors and increase cooperation toward sustainable tourism. Stafford-Smith noted that successful implementation of the SDGs requires collaboration between multiple stakeholders, including governments, civil society, and the private sector (Stafford-Smith et al., 2017). The role of blockchain technology in international development cooperation, including potential benefits and challenges, is essential (Aysan et al., 2021b). In addition, using smart contracts can reduce the need for intermediaries in international transactions, further streamline the process, and potentially reduce costs. Blockchain technology could enable the creation of decentralized markets for tourism services that can provide economic opportunities for local communities, promote responsible consumption and production, and increase transparency, efficiency, and trust in transactions and agreements. Such collaborations between stakeholders can contribute to achieving sustainable tourism goals by promoting sustainable tourism practices, improving the quality of life of local communities, and conserving natural resources (Benckendorff et al., 2009).

Blockchain and Smart Contracts

Blockchain is a distributed digital ledger technology that maintains secure, transparent, and unchangeable digital records (Önder & Treiblmaier, 2018). It utilizes a network of connected devices to decentralizedly verify and record transactions. The structure is known as a "blockchain" because each data block in the chain carries an encrypted message from the preceding block, forming a chain of safe blocks. This process guarantees that efforts to change data are discovered and denied by the network, protecting the system's integrity. To this aim, using consensus algorithms like "Proof of Work" or "Proof of Stake" ensures that all network stakeholders concur on the distributed ledger's final state, further enhancing the security and dependability of the system (Saad & Radzi, 2020).

A hash function is a mathematical function that maps input data of arbitrary size to a fixed-size output called a hash value. The hash function is a critical component of blockchain technology used to create digital fingerprints of data to verify the integrity of transactions. Hash functions are designed to be irreversible, meaning generating the original data from the hash value is impossible. This feature ensures data immutability on a blockchain and increases its security (Balistri et al., 2021).

Smart contracts are self-executing digital agreements that can facilitate, verify, or enforce the negotiation or execution of a deal without the need for intermediaries. Smart contracts are executed automatically when certain predefined conditions are met, such as a specific date or time, a specific event, or a trigger from an external data source. The logic of smart contracts is encoded in software code that is stored in a blockchain network and replicated across all nodes in the network. This feature ensures the transparency, security, and immutability of the contract, as well as the ability to automate complex business processes (Eggers et al., 2021). Figure 9.1 outlines the structure of the blockchain and its integration with smart contracts.

According to Triana et al., integrating blockchain and smart contracts enables transparent and decentralized transactions, reducing fraud and corruption and increasing stakeholder trust (Triana Casallas et al., 2020). Incorporating technologies such as blockchain and smart contracts could allow advanced sustainability practices in the tourism industry (Joo et al., 2021). Similarly, integrating smart contracts can reduce carbon emissions, enabling more efficient resource

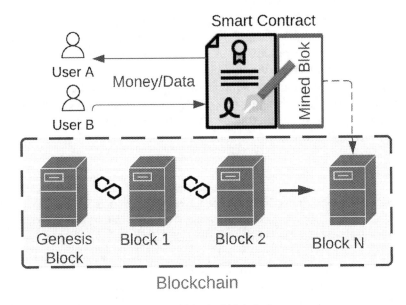

FIGURE 9.1 Use of smart contracts within the blockchain structure.

management and promoting sustainable practices (Dondjio, 2023; Esmaeilian et al., 2020). Hartmann and Thomas stated in their research that innovative contract-based carbon credit trading platforms will increase the transparency and traceability of carbon credit trading (Hartmann & Thomas, 2020). This could encourage more effective reductions of carbon emissions in the industry (Cheng, 2023; Farris et al., 2021).

Blockchain and smart contracts can potentially support sustainable energy use in tourism (Özgit & Adalıer, 2022). Smart contracts enable stakeholders to monitor, protect, and fairly allocate water use, one of the essential resources for ensuring sustainability (Grigoras et al., 2018). Furthermore, in increasing the transparency and efficiency of the human resource management system in the tourism industry, smart contracts also have the potential to create a sustainable workforce (Aghaei et al., 2021; Balasubramanian et al., 2022).

IoT and Sustainability

Integrating IoT devices can increase the effectiveness of tourist operations and provide real-time monitoring of social and environmental impact data. According to a study by Ulrich et al. (2022), incorporating the IoT into tourism can improve sustainability by optimizing resource management and cutting waste. By offering individualized waste reduction advice and real-time data on resource use, IoT integration in the tourist industry may encourage sustainable consumer behavior. IoT-enabled customized recommendations may persuade tourists to choose more environmentally friendly travel strategies, such as using transport and accommodations with lower energy usage (Belli et al., 2020; Verma et al., 2021).

IoT-based smart water management systems may also enhance sustainable water consumption practices and considerably lower water use in tourist locations (Vivek et al., 2020). IoT implementation can boost energy consumption in hotels, providing a competitive advantage and reducing expenses (Mercan et al., 2021). According to research results on the services of IoT-based waste management systems, related technologies can aid in pollution control by encouraging recycling habits and reducing remaining output (Fatimah et al., 2020).

Decentralized Finance "DeFi" and Tourism

Decentralized finance, or DeFi, is a novel financial system that eliminates intermediaries and is built on public blockchains like Ethereum. Decentralized exchanges, platforms for lending and borrowing funds, stablecoins trade, and other financing tools are all part of DeFi applications. These application systems are based on smart contracts, self-executing agreements operating on the blockchain network. DeFi aims to create more decentralized, open, and transparent financial options.

DeFi integration with smart contracts can enhance resource management, lower operating costs, and boost the security and transparency of tourism payments in tourism. For example, decentralized systems for the interaction of tourist service providers and clients can be built using blockchain-based smart contracts. Based on pre-established circumstances, transactions are executed automatically and transparently.

Smart contracts can boost payment efficiency, decrease fraud, promote transparency, and enhance security for service providers, according to a study by Lee et al. (2021). By giving investors a decentralized financing option that allows them to fund initiatives consistent with their ideas and sustainability objectives, DeFi can aid in developing sustainable tourist ventures. DeFi can also realize sustainable investments and financing models, such as green bonds or impact investing, that can support sustainable tourism initiatives. Samadhiya et al. (2023) have shown that blockchain technology can improve sustainable management by enabling real-time monitoring of natural resource consumption, reducing operational costs, and increasing transparency. Similarly, Radović et al. (2020) note that appropriate funding can facilitate sustainable tourism financing and investment and promote environmental protection.

By automating financial processes and ensuring compliance with sustainability standards with DeFi, blockchain-based smart contracts can increase transparency, accountability, and confidence in sustainable tourism investments. These technologies can reduce the need for intermediaries, creating cost savings and increased efficiency. For this reason, DeFi addresses a technologically critical condition in the tourism industry with its developing usage areas and constitutes a different dimension of leveraging technological innovations for sustainable development.

Blockchain technology could create a decentralized tourism ecosystem where tourists can directly interact with local communities and engage in sustainable activities such as eco-tourism or cultural exchange programs. DeFi can encourage adopting sustainable tourism practices by incentivizing businesses and individuals that comply with environmental and social standards, leading to the long-term conservation of natural and cultural resources. The research questions that may arise from the use of decentralized financial systems and smart contracts in the funding of sustainable tourism are as follows:

1 How can blockchain technology and smart contracts be used to advance sustainable tourism finance?
2 What are the main challenges in implementing blockchain-based smart contracts in sustainable tourism finance, and how can they be addressed?
3 How can blockchain-based smart contracts increase transparency and accountability in sustainable tourism finance?
4 What is the potential impact of blockchain-based smart contracts on the sustainability of tourism development?
5 How can blockchain-based smart contracts facilitate sustainable investment and financing in tourism?
6 What are the potential economic, social, and environmental benefits of using blockchain-based smart contracts in sustainable tourism finance?
7 What are the ethical implications of using blockchain-based smart contracts in sustainable tourism finance, and how can they be addressed?
8 How can blockchain-based smart contracts contribute to achieving the United Nations SDGs in the tourism sector?
9 How can blockchain-based smart contracts in sustainable tourism finance be scaled to a broader range of stakeholders and destinations?
10 What are the potential barriers and challenges need to be addressed to successfully implement blockchain-based smart contracts in sustainable tourism finance?
11 How can blockchain-based smart contracts be used to promote sustainable tourism practices among tourists and local communities?
12 What are the social and economic impacts of using blockchain-based smart contracts in sustainable tourism finance, and how can they be managed to ensure fair and inclusive outcomes?

Applying blockchain-based smart contracts in sustainable tourism, Bodkhe et al. have developed a blockchain-based smart contract system for sustainable tourism financing and proposed a model that allows tourists to interact with various stakeholders through a single digital wallet identifier to initiate payments (Bodkhe et al., 2019). In the Li (2019) study, blockchain reliability, performance, efficiency, privacy, auditing, and online-offline integration were examined within the scope of

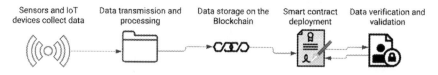

FIGURE 9.2   Connection of blockchain-based smart contracts with environmental data in tourism enterprises.

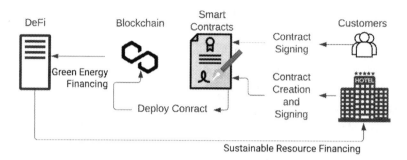

FIGURE 9.3   Interrelationship between decentralized financial systems with smart contracts.

the redesign. It is important to involve stakeholders in the redesign and iteration process to address their needs and issues (Darwish et al., 2023).

In sustainable tourism finance, Figure 9.2 indicates the basic operating logic of the blockchain structure, connected between the values obtained from the environmental data of the tourism enterprise and the IoT devices with smart contracts. It shows the basic infrastructure in the developed model of ecological data for tourism enterprises associated with smart contracts connected to the blockchain.

Smart contracts will be able to develop solutions to create designs that meet the sector's needs and the newly developing decentralized financial needs. Figure 9.3 indicates the association of agreements created between the hotel and customers with decentralized economic systems and smart contracts. The contracts to be made for this purpose will be able to connect tourism enterprises with customers with arrangements to be created automatically and establish a link that can be placed in this structure with the decentralized financial systems.

DeFi has the potential to address various sustainability challenges, including reducing carbon emissions, promoting renewable energy, ensuring fair trade, and supporting social and economic development. Blockchain technologies can be applied in sustainable finance, green energy, and sustainable agriculture investment to create more transparent, efficient, and decentralized systems that ensure trust and accountability between all parties involved in sustainability practices.

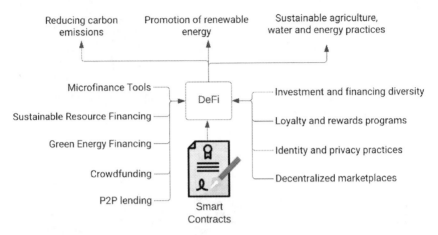

FIGURE 9.4 The relationship between the decentralized financial system and smart contracts.

In addition, DeFi can facilitate the development of innovative financing mechanisms such as micro-finance, crowdfunding, and peer-to-peer (P2P) lending that can empower local communities and businesses to access financing and resources that support sustainability goals (Zetzsche et al., 2020). Figure 9.4 outlines the links between decentralized financial structures and smart contracts.

Added values within the scope of the decentralized financial system can be summarized as follows:

- Payment and money transfers: DeFi makes it possible to construct instant and low-cost payments and money transfers between tourists and tourism service providers without intermediaries such as banks.
- Investment and financing: DeFi can offer new opportunities for tourism enterprises to obtain funding through decentralized platforms and allow investors to invest directly in tourism projects.
- Loyalty and rewards programs: It can help create decentralized loyalty and rewards programs, unlike traditional programs that are transparent and secure.
- Identity: It can enable the creation of decentralized identity systems that can verify the identities and data of tourists and protect their privacy.
- Decentralized marketplaces: DeFi can create decentralized marketplaces that connect tourists with local hosts and service providers without intermediaries.

Thanks to its traceable transactions, smart contracts and decentralized financial structures can provide an infrastructure to meet improved funding needs. For this purpose, the necessary financing and money transfers to meet sustainable goals can be supplied in decentralized structures.

Decentralized funding can also improve the network of access to the new financial resources that tourism businesses need for sustainable investments. In terms of sustainability, the scalability of investors in this context can ensure the follow-up of their investments with a data set. In addition to traditional financial instruments, the combination of resources provided by decentralized systems can create additional income for the sustainable financing needed. Various reward programs and decentralized marketplaces to be designed can be integrated with this infrastructure to meet financing needs.

Conclusion

In achieving sustainable tourism goals, smart contracts and decentralized financial services created by newly developed blockchain technologies that have found application in many areas can contribute to realizing SDGs. In this context, the most crucial contribution provided by technology is that the stakeholders in sustainability goals can create added value within the decentralized structure. For this purpose, it is necessary to identify the main success factors for technological adaptation, develop policy recommendations, make essential predictions for the industry, and measure the contributions to sustainable development to increase trust and accountability. In transforming technologies, sustainable tourism practices should also be encouraged to stakeholders with common platforms on data privacy and security improvements.

The smart contracts that emerge with blockchain technologies and decentralized financial solutions can contribute to SDGs. Encrypting environmental data and controlling it in decentralized structures and ensuring the joint participation of stakeholders with contracts based on these structures can create significant added value in monitoring sustainability. Blockchain's successful application in energy, water, and waste management reveals that smart contracts will create added value for the tourism industry. In this context, by combining environmental data with smart contracts and decentralized financing systems, an ecosystem can be made so that ecological awareness creates added value for all stakeholders.

Platforms and models using design-based research methods can be developed with industry stakeholders to facilitate blockchain technologies in the tourism sector. Smart contracts should be designed to create added value for all stakeholders, and in this context, decentralized financial needs should be auditable on a common platform. For smart contracts to better contribute to sustainable tourism, the implementation and testing process should also be designed according to the feedback of sector stakeholders.

References

Aghaei, H., Naderibeni, N., & Karimi, A. (2021). Designing a tourism business model on block chain platform. *Tourism Management Perspectives, 39*, 100845.

Al Sadawi, A., Madani, B., Saboor, S., Ndiaye, M., &. Abu-Lebdeh, G. (2021). A comprehensive hierarchical blockchain system for carbon emission trading utilizing blockchain of things and smart contract. *Technological Forecasting and Social Change, 173*, 121124.

Ali, A., Rasoolimanesh, S. M., & Cobanoglu, C. (2020). Technology in tourism and hospitality to achieve Sustainable Development Goals (SDGs). *Journal of Hospitality and Tourism Technology, 11*(2), 177–181.

Aysan, A. F., Bergigui, F., & Disli, M. (2021a). Blockchain-based solutions in achieving SDGs after COVID-19. *Journal of Open Innovation: Technology, Market, and Complexity, 7*(2), 151.

Aysan, A. F., Bergigui, F., & Dişli, M. (2021b). Using blockchain-enabled solutions as SDG accelerators in the international development space. *Sustainability, 13*(7), 4025.

Azmat, M., & Thanou, E. (2023). Blockchain-enabled smart contract architecture in supply chain design. In *Blockchain Driven Supply Chain Management* (pp. 1–14). Springer Singapore.

Balasubramanian, S., Sethi, J. S., Ajayan, S., & Paris, C. M. (2022). An enabling framework for blockchain in tourism. *Information Technology & Tourism, 24*(2), 165–179.

Balistri, E., Casellato, F., Giannelli, C., & Stefanelli, C. (2021). BlockHealth: Blockchain-based secure and peer-to-peer health information sharing with data protection and right to be forgotten. *ICT Express, 7*(3), 308–315.

Belli, L., Cilfone, A., Davoli, L., Ferrari, G., Adorni, P., Di Nocera, F., ... & Bertolotti, E. (2020). IoT-enabled smart sustainable cities: Challenges and approaches. *Smart Cities, 3*(3), 1039–1071.

Benckendorff, P., Edwards, D., Jurowski, C., Liburd, J. J., Miller, G., & Moscardo, G. (2009). Exploring the future of tourism and quality of life. *Tourism and Hospitality Research, 9*(2), 171–183.

Bexell, M., & Jönsson, K. (2017). Responsibility and the United Nations' sustainable development goals. In *Forum for Development Studies* (Vol. 44, No. 1, pp. 13–29). Routledge.

Bodkhe, U., Bhattacharya, P., Tanwar, S., Tyagi, S., Kumar, N., & Obaidat, M. S. (2019). BloHosT: Blockchain enabled smart tourism and hospitality management. In *2019 International Conference on Computer, Information and Telecommunication Systems (CITS)* (pp. 1–5). IEEE.

Boluk, K. A., Cavaliere, C. T., &. Higgins-Desbiolles, F. (2019). A critical framework for interrogating the United Nations Sustainable Development Goals 2030 Agenda in tourism. *Journal of Sustainable Tourism, 27*, 847–864.

Brundtland, G. H. (1987). *Report of the World Commission on Environment and Development: "Our Common Future"*. FLOUR.

Cheng, R. (2023). Assessing and validating tourism business model in hospitality industry: Role of blockchain platform. *Environmental Science and Pollution Research, 30*, 63704–63715.

Ćirić, Z., & Ivanišević, S. (2018). Blockchain and tourism development: Case of Malta. *Modern Management Tools and Economy of Tourism Sector in Present Era*, 565. 3rd International Thematic Monograph.

Darwish, A., Lindman, J., Hjertqvist, J., & Tona, O. (2023). *Design Principles for Blockchain-Based Applications in Green Bond Reporting*. Proceedings of the 56th Hawaii International Conference on System Sciences, pp. 5186–5195.

de Villiers, C., Kuruppu, S., & Dissanayake, D. (2021). A (new) role for business–Promoting the United Nations' Sustainable Development Goals through the internet-of-things and blockchain technology. *Journal of Business Research, 131*, 598–609.

Demirel, E., Karagoz Zeren, S., & Hakan, K. (2022). Smart contracts in tourism industry: A model with blockchain integration for post pandemic economy. *Current Issues in Tourism, 25*(12), 1895–1909.

Di Vaio, A., & Varriale, L. (2020). Blockchain technology in supply chain management for sustainable performance: Evidence from the airport industry. *International Journal of Information Management, 52*, 102014.

Dondjio, I. (2023). The importance of blockchain for ecomobility in smart cities: A systematic literature review. In *Information Systems: 19th European, Mediterranean, and Middle Eastern Conference, EMCIS 2022, Virtual Event, December 21–22, 2022, Proceedings* (pp. 165–184). Springer Nature Switzerland.

Eggers, J., Hein, A., Weking, J., Bohm, M., & Krcmar, H. (2021). Process automation on the blockchain: An exploratory case study on smart contracts. Proceedings of the 54th Hawaii International Conference on System Sciences, pp. 5607–5616

El Khatib, M., Beshwari, F., Beshwari, M., & Beshwari, A. (2021). The impact of block-chain on project management. *ICIC Express Lett, 15*(5), 467–474.

Esmaeilian, B., Sarkis, J., Lewis, K., & Behdad, S. (2020). Blockchain for the future of sustainable supply chain management in Industry 4.0. *Resources, Conservation and Recycling, 163*, 105064.

Farris, G., Pinna, A., Baralla, G., Tonelli, R., Modica, P., & Marchesi, M. (2021). Design of a blockchain-oriented system for the sustainable disintermediation in tourism. In *2021 IoT Vertical and Topical Summit for Tourism* (pp. 1–6). IEEE.

Fatimah, Y. A., Govindan, K., Murniningsih, R., & Setiawan, A. (2020). Industry 4.0 based sustainable circular economy approach for smart waste management system to achieve sustainable development goals: A case study of Indonesia. *Journal of Cleaner Production, 269*, 122263.

Fonseca, L. M., Domingues, J. P., & Dima, A. M. (2020). Mapping the sustainable development goals relationships. *Sustainability, 12*(8), 3359.

Ghahremani-Nahr, J., Aliahmadi, A., & Nozari, H. (2022). An IoT-based sustainable supply chain framework and blockchain. *International Journal of Innovation in Engineering, 2*(1), 12–21.

Goodland, R., & Daly, H. (1996). Environmental sustainability: Universal and non-negotiable. *Ecological Applications, 6*(4), 1002–1017.

Graci, S. (2013). Collaboration and partnership development for sustainable tourism. *Tourism Geographies, 15*(1), 25–42.

Grigoras, G., Bison, N., Enescu, F. M., Guede, J. M. L., Salado, G. F., Brennan, R., ... & Alalm, M. G. (2018). ICT based smart management solution to realize water and energy savings through energy efficiency measures in water distribution systems. In *2018 10th International Conference on Electronics, Computers and Artificial Intelligence (ECAI)* (pp. 1–4). IEEE.

Hartmann, S., & Thomas, S. (2020). Applying blockchain to the Australian carbon market. *Economic Papers: A Journal of Applied Economics and Policy, 39*(2), 133–151.

Joo, J., Park, J., & Han, Y. (2021). Applications of blockchain and smart contract for sustainable tourism ecosystems. In *Evolutionary Computing and Mobile Sustainable Networks: Proceedings of ICECMSN 2020* (pp. 773–780). Springer Singapore.

Kahya, A., Avyukt, A., Ramachandran, G. S., & Krishnamachari, B. (2021). Blockchain-enabled personalized incentives for sustainable behavior in smart cities. In *2021 International Conference on Computer Communications and Networks (ICCCN)* (pp. 1–6). IEEE.

Kim, S. K., & Huh, J. H. (2020). Blockchain of carbon trading for UN sustainable development goals. *Sustainability, 12*(10), 4021.

Lee, D. K. C., Yan, L., & Wang, Y. (2021). A global perspective on central bank digital currency. *China Economic Journal, 14*(1), 52–66.

Li, Y. (2019). Emerging blockchain-based applications and techniques. *Service Oriented Computing and Applications, 13*, 279–285.

Madanaguli, A., Dhir, A., Joseph, R. P., Albishri, N. A., & Srivastava, S. (2023). Environmental sustainability practices and strategies in the rural tourism and hospitality sector: A systematic literature review and suggestions for future research. *Scandinavian Journal of Hospitality and Tourism, 23*(1), 1–28.

Mavilia, R., & Pisani, R. (2020). Blockchain and catching-up in developing countries: The case of financial inclusion in Africa. *African Journal of Science, Technology, Innovation and Development, 12*(2), 151–163.

Mercan, S., Cain, L., Akkaya, K., Cebe, M., Uluağaç, S., Alonso, M., & Çobanoğlu, C. (2021). Improving the service industry with hyper-connectivity: IoT in hospitality. *International Journal of Contemporary Hospitality Management, 33*(1), 243–262.

Mishra, L., & Kaushik, V. (2021). Application of blockchain in dealing with sustainability issues and challenges of the financial sector. *Journal of Sustainable Finance & Investment, 13*(3), 1–16.

Nam, K., Dutt, C. S., Chathoth, P., & Khan, M. S. (2021). Blockchain technology for smart city and smart tourism: Latest trends and challenges. *Asia Pacific Journal of Tourism Research, 26*(4), 454–468.

Negi, D., Shah, A., Rawat, S., Choudhury, T., & Khanna, A. (2021). Block chain platforms and smart contracts. In *Blockchain Applications in IoT Ecosystem* (pp. 65–76). Springer International Publishing.

Önder, I., & Treiblmaier, H. (2018). Blockchain and tourism: Three research propositions. *Annals of Tourism Research, 72*(C), 180–182.

Opoku, A. (2016). SDG2030: A sustainable built environment's role in achieving the post-2015 United Nations Sustainable Development Goals. In *Proceedings of the 32nd Annual ARCOM Conference* (Vol. 2, pp. 1149–1158). Association of Researchers in Construction Management.

Özgit, H., & Adalıer, A. (2022). Can blockchain technology help small islands achieve sustainable tourism? A perspective on North Cyprus. *Worldwide Hospitality and Tourism Themes* (ahead-of-print), *14*(4), 374–383.

Ozkan, E., Azizi, N., & Haass, O. (2021). Leveraging smart contract in project procurement through DLT to gain sustainable competitive advantages. *Sustainability, 13*(23), 13380.

Pan, Y., Zhang, X., Wang, Y., Yan, J., Zhou, S., Li, G., & Bao, J. (2019). Application of blockchain in carbon trading. *Energy Procedia, 158*, 4286–4291.

Parmentola, A., Petrillo, A., Tutore, I., & De Felice, F. (2022). Is blockchain able to enhance environmental sustainability? A systematic review and research agenda from the perspective of Sustainable Development Goals (SDGs). *Business Strategy and the Environment, 31*(1), 194–217.

Pinna, A., & Ibba, S. (2019). A blockchain-based decentralized system for proper handling of temporary employment contracts. In *Intelligent Computing: Proceedings of the 2018 Computing Conference* (Vol. 2, pp. 1231–1243). Springer International Publishing.

Pradhan, N. R., & Singh, A. P. (2021). Smart contracts for automated control system in blockchain-based smart cities. *Journal of Ambient Intelligence and Smart Environments, 13*(3), 253–267.

Radović, G., Petrović, M. D., Demirović Bajrami, D., Radovanović, M., & Vuković, N. (2020). Can proper funding enhance sustainable tourism in rural settings? Evidence from a developing country. *Sustainability, 12*(18), 7797.

Rashideh, W. (2020). Blockchain technology framework: Current and future perspectives for the tourism industry. *Tourism Management, 80,* 104125.

Saad, S. M. S., & Radzi, R. Z. R. M. (2020). Comparative review of the blockchain consensus algorithm between proof of stake (PoS) and delegated proof of stake (DPoS). *International Journal of Innovative Computing, 10*(2), 27–32.

Saberi, S., Kouhizadeh, M., Sarkis, J., & Shen, L. (2019). Blockchain technology and its relationships to sustainable supply chain management. *International Journal of Production Research, 57*(7), 2117–2135.

Samadhiya, A., Agrawal, R., Kumar, A., & Garza-Reyes, J. A. (2023). Blockchain technology and circular economy in the environment of total productive maintenance: A natural resource-based view perspective. *Journal of Manufacturing Technology Management* (ahead-of-print), *34*(2), 293–314.

Saraji, S., & Borowczak, M. (2021). A blockchain-based carbon credit ecosystem. arXiv preprint arXiv:2107.00185.

Sivarethinamohan, R., & Sujatha, S. (2021). Unraveling the potential of artificial intelligence-driven blockchain technology in environment management. In *Advances in Mechanical Engineering: Select Proceedings of CAMSE 2020* (pp. 693–700). Springer Singapore.

Stafford-Smith, M., Griggs, D., Gaffney, O., Ullah, F., Reyers, B., Kanie, N., ... & O'Connell, D.(2017). Integration: The key to implementing the Sustainable Development Goals. *Sustainability Science, 12,* 911–919.

Triana Casallas, J. A., Cueva Lovelle, J. M., & Rodríguez Molano, J. I. (2020). Smart contracts with blockchain in the public sector. *International Journal of Interactive Multimedia and Artificial Intelligence, 6*(3), 63–72.

Tyan, I., Yagüe, M. I., & Guevara-Plaza, A. (2021). Blockchain technology's potential for sustainable tourism. In *Information and Communication Technologies in Tourism 2021: Proceedings of the ENTER 2021 eTourism Conference, January 19–22, 2021* (pp. 17–29). Springer International Publishing.

Ulrich, A. M. D., Reino, K., & Hjalager, A. M. (2022). Innovative internet of things (IoT) for sustainable tourism. In *Handbook of Innovation for Sustainable Tourism* (pp. 61–81). Edward Elgar Publishing.

UN DESA. (2022). *The Sustainable Development Goals Report 2022 - July 2022.* UN DESA. © UN DESA. https://unstats.un.org/sdgs/report/2022/.

UNWTO. (2021). Tourism and the sustainable development goals – Journey to 2030. Retrieved from: https://www.unwto.org/tourism-sustainable-development-goals.

Upadhyay, A., Mukhuty, S., Kumar, V., & Kazancoglu, Y. (2021). Blockchain technology and the circular economy: Implications for sustainability and social responsibility. *Journal of Cleaner Production, 293,* 126130.

Verma, A., Shukla, V. K., & Sharma, R. (2021). Convergence of IOT in tourism industry: A pragmatic analysis. *Journal of Physics: Conference Series, 1714*(1), 012037.

Vivek, K., Jain, L. K., Agarwal, A., Meher, S. S., Dhar, A., & Pramod, G. (2020). Review of smart water management techniques across the globe. https://www.researchgate.net/profile/Shyam-Meher/publication/354365088_Review_of_Smart_Water_Management_Techniques_across_the_globe/links/6138fd1da3a397270a8f16dc/Review-of-Smart-Water-Management-Techniques-across-the-globe.pdf

Weaver, D., & Faulkner, B. (2000). Sustainable tourism: Is it sustainable? In Williams, S. (Ed.), *Tourism: Tourism, develeopment and sustainability* (pp. 300–311). Milton Park, Abingdon: Taylor & Francis.

Whitaker, M., & Pawar, P. (2020). Commodity ecology: A virtual community platform for promoting responsible consumption and production to achieve SDG# 12. In *2020 IEEE Green Technologies Conference (GreenTech)* (pp. 59–61). IEEE.

Yeasmin, S., & Baig, A. (2019). Unblocking the potential of blockchain. In *2019 International Conference on Electrical and Computing Technologies and Applications (ICECTA)* (pp. 1–5). IEEE.

Zetzsche, D. A., Arner, D. W., & Buckley, R. P. (2020). Decentralized finance. *Journal of Financial Regulation, 6*(2), 172–203.

10

THE FUTURE OF BLOCKCHAIN TECHNOLOGY FOR TOURISM AND HOSPITALITY

Ulrike Gretzel

> We tend to overestimate the effect of a technology in the short run and underestimate the effect in the long run.
>
> *Amara's Law*

Looking into the future requires a solid understanding of the past and present. This is especially important for technologies that, like blockchain technology, are complex, that are still emerging, that have many application areas, and that are subject to a lot of media reporting (both in positive and negative terms). The Gartner Hype Cycle for Blockchain and Web3, 2022 (Litan, 2022) shows that some blockchain-related technologies are at the "peak of inflated expectations", while others have made it through the "trough of disillusionment"; however, none have reached the "plateau of productivity" as of yet. Blockchain technology is clearly gaining traction and has moved on from early, experimental stages to real-world applications that are adopted and exploited by an increasing number and a growing variety of users. It seems to have also emancipated itself from being used synonymously with cryptocurrencies and all the risks, booms and busts, and illegal activities they have been associated with.

This is also true for tourism and hospitality, where blockchain technology is increasingly used beyond offering cryptocurrency payment options. For instance, Revfine (n.d.) reports (as do many others) that TUI has implemented a blockchain application that allows it to move inventories between different points of sale in real time. It also lists examples of blockchain-based platforms that represent new marketplaces for hospitality products. Besides the in-house efforts by tourism players to seize the advantages of blockchain technology and the technology companies that are developing their own applications for tourism, companies that help tourism and hospitality providers develop blockchain apps and related

DOI: 10.4324/9781003351917-10

technologies are emerging, such as Appinventiv. There are also non-fungible token marketplaces and consulting companies like Nimi that work with museums to tap into the token economy (Treiblmaier, 2021). These new industry players will help small businesses, non-profits, and government organizations get access to customized blockchain solutions without having to invest in technical know-how. These new blockchain technology service offerings represent the beginnings of a blockchain-focused digital ecosystem. These solution providers also lend blockchain technology legitimacy and will serve as catalysts for further development and adoption within tourism and hospitality. In contrast to other technologies, like social media platforms or lateral exchange markets (Perren & Kozinets, 2018) that were exclusively developed outside of the industry, blockchain technology-related change seems to be driven by developments outside the industry but also within and around the core tourism and hospitality industry.

The ideas behind blockchain technology have proven themselves to be extremely useful, and in many ways "game-changing". The blockchain technology "genie" is out of the bottle and it is difficult to imagine a future that will not, in some way or shape, be based on blockchain technology. Taking a longitudinal perspective that extrapolates from the past, it is also clear that there will be many iterations of the technology and even more innovative applications. The blockchain technology of the future will not look like the blockchain technology of the past, but its underlying principles and basic affordances will change expectations and approaches forever.

What is also important is contextual understanding. The tourism and hospitality context is very particular in that it involves a myriad of stakeholders and simultaneously exhibits technology affinity and aversion. Indeed, there are some reports of tourism and hospitality lagging behind other industries in terms of blockchain technology adoption (Thees, Erschbamer, & Pechlaner, 2020). On the other hand, tourism and hospitality is a very information-intense context, with decentralization in many areas and heavy intermediation in others, with complex data and money flows, with high risks and low trust (Werthner & Klein, 1999). Much of tourism happens across borders, which means that there are also elaborate flows of travelers, workers and goods that need verification and processing across different kinds of systems and regulatory environments. Further, the global COVID-19 pandemic fueled digitalization in the tourism and hospitality industry and helped close the diffusion of innovation chasm for several technologies (Gretzel et al., 2020). These are all factors that generally favor blockchain adoption. Irannezhad and Mahadevan (2021) go so far as to suggest that blockchain technology might provide tourism and hospitality with "new hope" (p. 85) in the aftermath of the COVID-19 pandemic.

However, while it is possible to make informed guesses about the future of blockchain technology in tourism and hospitality, this chapter will also raise questions about the kind of blockchain future these different stakeholders would like to see and whether they will have an opportunity to actively shape it. Blockchain technology's disruption potential in tourism and hospitality is tremendous and involves both incremental and radical innovation that will lead to new players entering the industry, new business models adopted by incumbent firms, and more subtle but extensive changes enabled by the widespread adoption of blockchain technology applications by existing stakeholders, including governments and consumers (Zach, Nicolau, & Sharma, 2020).

To provide a basic framework for thinking about the future of blockchain technology in tourism and hospitality, this chapter will first briefly overview the premises and promises of blockchain technology to facilitate analyzing and imagining its potential. More detailed explanations are available in other chapters and in the fast-growing literature on blockchain technology in tourism and hospitality (e.g., in Antoniadis, Spinthiropoulos, & Kontsas, 2020; Kwok & Koh, 2019; Önder & Gunter, 2022; Önder & Treiblmaier, 2018; Rashideh, 2020; Thees et al., 2020; Treiblmaier, 2020; Valeri & Baggio, 2021). The chapter will then focus on three particular contexts or scenarios within tourism and hospitality that provide particular opportunities but also important challenges for blockchain technology development and implementation.

Overview of Blockchain Technology and Its Relevance in Tourism and Hospitality

Blockchain technology records and tracks transactions securely and transparently. It creates a permanent, unalterable, and tamper-proof record of transactions that can be shared and retrieved in real time without a centralized authority or intermediary. Blockchain technology is a type of distributed ledger technology (Maull et al., 2017). Each transaction is recorded as a "block", validated by a network of computers (nodes), and added to a chain of previous blocks (hence the name blockchain). This process records network transactions chronologically and permanently. In a blockchain network, nodes typically use a proof-of-work (PoW) or proof-of-stake (PoS) consensus mechanism to validate transactions and add blocks to the chain (Treiblmaier, 2020). Blockchain applications (e.g., cryptocurrencies, smart contracts, tokens) often combine several innovative technologies or computing approaches, meaning they are complex technological assemblages. For a detailed overview of blockchain technologies, see Lacity and Treiblmaier (2022).

The main advantages of blockchain technology are its decentralized approach to validating transactions and the fact that it creates a tamper-proof and immutable ledger by cryptographically linking each block in a blockchain to the previous block. These characteristics create transparency, accountability, and trust. Because blockchain technology can automate processes and reduce the time and cost associated with manual record-keeping and verification, it can also increase efficiency and reduce the risk of errors. These advantages of blockchain technology have been highlighted repeatedly by existing literature (see Calvaresi et al., 2019) and have been translated into specific application areas for tourism and hospitality, ranging from inventory management to digital payments, fund-raising, and personalized marketing (Önder & Gunter, 2022; Tham & Sigala, 2020; Treiblmaier, 2020). Another important advantage of blockchain technology is its promise of disintermediation (Önder & Treiblmaier, 2018), which is certainly a welcome prospect in tourism and hospitality, where complex value chains and powerful, global intermediaries continue to dominate.

Balasubramanian et al. (2022) suggest that blockchain technology does not only simplify operations and coordination within the tourism and hospitality industry, but also has major implications across all stages and types of tourism and hospitality experiences. Blockchain technology is a building block for many efforts seeking to make tourism and hospitality experiences more seamless but also more personalized and memorable. However, most contemporary blockchain technology applications are implemented "behind-the-scenes" and awareness and knowledge of blockchain technology (beyond cryptocurrencies) remain rather low in the general population (Raddatz et al., 2023).

There is no doubt that blockchain technology has spurred innovation activity and will continue to inspire a multitude of innovations for tourism and hospitality. However, general innovation deficiencies in tourism and hospitality (Hjalager, 2002) continue to prevail and will certainly also damper many of the innovative blockchain-related efforts. The most promising avenues for blockchain technology development in tourism and hospitality seem to be in conjunction with broader initiatives that critically rely on many of the benefits blockchain technology provides. Three of these initiatives will therefore be discussed in this chapter: smart tourism, the Metaverse, and sustainable tourism.

The Future of Blockchain Technology in Smart Tourism

Smart tourism represents a paradigm shift in the way that tourism is conceptualized and managed (Gretzel et al., 2015a). Smart tourism is a form of tourism development that takes advantage of advanced technologies to envision and realize destinations in which tourists and residents alike benefit from enhanced experiential offerings (Gretzel & Koo, 2021). At the same time, it implements new forms of governance models to ensure that sustainable development goals are achieved (Soares et al., 2022). One of its major components is a digital business ecosystem that fosters innovation (Gretzel et al., 2015b). The flexible interplay of various value-creating entities within this digital business ecosystem results in smartness at the destination level. Triple-helix partnerships (between research institutions, public bodies, and private enterprises) (Ruuska & Teigland, 2009) constitute the lifeblood of this smart tourism ecosystem and ensure that hard and soft smartness components are developed and implemented across the smart destination (Boes, Buhalis, & Inversini, 2016).

Although smart tourism is often hailed for its desired outcomes (sustainability, accessibility/inclusivity, creativity/innovation, and digitalization), it is really the processes behind smart tourism that make it a promising tool to achieve change in tourism. Gretzel, Ham, and Koo (2018) explain that these processes happen across various layers in smart destinations. In the physical layer, technology infrastructure is built to digitalize the physical world. This phygital layer contains a variety of devices and sensor technologies, which produce and communicate data. The data layer of smart destinations consolidates and monitors data. On top of this data layer sits a business layer, which translates data into technology-supported value offerings. The governance layer of smart tourism coordinates efforts within the smart destination and provides governance mechanisms to ensure that these value offerings are consistent with smart tourism goals. Notions of "good governance", justice, and participatory governance come into play in this layer to establish and inform processes and guide decision-making (Gretzel & Jamal, 2020). All these layers together support the experience layer in which residents and tourists encounter enhanced, technology-augmented experiences (Gretzel & Koo, 2021; Neuhofer, Buhalis, & Ladkin, 2014).

Mapping the capabilities and potential benefits of blockchain technology onto the layers of smart destinations and smart tourism goals reveals the many ways in which blockchain technology supports smart tourism initiatives. Smart tourism requires large infrastructure projects, and blockchain technology can support such complex projects across their financing, project management, compliance, and general coordination needs. Smart energy grids and sensor networks can also benefit from blockchain technology's ability to create efficiency in complex systems. Within the data layer, blockchain technology can help overcome data quality, ownership, and privacy issues that often plague smart tourism initiatives. In the business layer, blockchain technology can facilitate cooperatition and encourage innovation through its many applications. It can also help manage intellectual property rights in triple-helix innovation efforts. In the governance layer, blockchain technology can help establish secure voting systems that enable participation of various actors. It can also help with automating monitoring and coordination. At the experience layer, so-called DApps (decentralized applications) promise the availability of new experiences. Nam et al. (2021) list a number of applications that have already been developed for smart tourism purposes.

Smart tourism initiatives have received major funding around the world. Although some of the more ambitious projects have failed (especially those in which large tech companies tried to hijack smart tourism ideas for their own purposes), post-pandemic tourism has renewed interest in destination-wide solutions and has created renewed urgency to change existing approaches to destination management, especially visitor monitoring and management. The symbiosis between smart tourism and blockchain technology is evident. Future smart tourism efforts will increasingly rely on blockchain technology for their successful implementation, while blockchain technology development will benefit from the investments made in smart tourism and the innovation activities of digital business ecosystems with their triple-helix research and development partnerships.

The Future of Blockchain Technology in the Metaverse

The term Metaverse describes a collective virtual space that is created by the convergence of multiple virtual and physical realities. The resulting network of interconnected virtual and augmented worlds blurs the boundaries between the physical and the virtual. It enables users to interact in new ways with each other, with artifacts, with brands or other organizations, and with places. The Metaverse offers not only new opportunities for interactions but also possibilities for commerce and for the exploration of phygital spaces. The major premises of the Metaverse are that it is an open, hardware-agnostic, persistent, collective space that offers experiences that are immersive, synchronous, shared, spatial, and consumed through an avatar or some other continuous and visual representation of identity.

The Metaverse is often conceptualized as a new digital frontier and a new iteration of the Internet. It creates opportunities for innovation, creativity, and ubiquitous value (co-)creation. In the tourism and hospitality context, it has been portrayed as a disruptive innovation with enormous potential to support experiences across all trip stages and with critical capabilities to facilitate a variety of tourism marketing and management processes and offerings (Buhalis, Leung, & Lin, 2023; Yang & Wang, 2023). The development of the Metaverse is driven by recent advancements in virtual reality technology and artificial intelligence, and is supported by a number of other emerging technologies, including blockchain technology.

Blockchain technology supports the Metaverse in a number of critical ways. Overall, blockchain technology can provide a secure, transparent, and efficient infrastructure for the Metaverse, allowing for the creation and exchange of virtual assets, the establishment of a decentralized governance system, and the development of a secure payment system. Specifically, blockchain technology can be utilized to establish ownership and provenance of virtual assets, including virtual real estate, digital artwork, and in-game objects. Additionally, blockchain technology can provide a secure and transparent method for Metaverse users to trade and exchange these assets. The Metaverse will also require a governance system to administer various aspects of its network of virtual worlds, including the creation and management of virtual assets, the resolution of disputes, and the enforcement of rules and regulations. Blockchain technology can facilitate such a transparent and user-responsible decentralized governance system.

Moreover, the Metaverse will require a secure and efficient payment system to facilitate user-to-user transactions, such as the purchase of virtual or augmented products and services. Blockchain technology can provide a fraud- and hacker-resistant, secure, and transparent payment system to fuel the Metaverse economy. The identity verification function of blockchain technology will also be important as users will want to control their own data and defend their privacy within the Metaverse. Last, but not least, since the Metaverse is anticipated to include multiple virtual worlds and platforms, blockchain technology can provide a standard for interoperability between these disparate systems, allowing for seamless integration.

While the overall vision of the Metaverse is far from being realized, many of its aspects have been developed and are increasingly adopted by companies and users. Tourism and hospitality-affine industries like museums and theme parks, gaming and entertainment, art and fashion, and meetings and events are increasingly exploring Metaverse applications to augment their offerings. Much of this development is happening in Asia and in conjunction with smart tourism efforts (see, for example, Um et al., 2022). While smart tourism connects the physical and the digital world, the Metaverse adds a virtual layer on top that supports the smart tourism business ecosystem as well as the smart tourist experience (Gretzel et al., 2015b). Blockchain technology will serve as an important building block in the realization of smart Metaverse tourism. In summary, blockchain technology is the glue that holds the Metaverse together and will therefore play a core role in its future development. With increasing investment in the Metaverse, the importance of blockchain technology will certainly grow in tandem.

The Future of Blockchain Technology in Sustainable Tourism

An area that has received comparatively less attention is blockchain technology's potential applications in the context of sustainable tourism. Smart tourism also acknowledges sustainability as one of its major pillars (Gretzel et al., 2015a) but has a different approach toward achieving it. While smart tourism embraces governance, collaboration, and consensus, blockchain-driven sustainable tourism adopts a neoliberal approach toward achieving sustainable development goals through responsibilization of consumers (Giesler & Veresiu, 2014) and the glorification of markets. The anti-government ethos of Silicon Valley and the idolization of wealth are ingrained in everything that blockchain technology is and stands for. Rather than agreeing on regulation and common goals, blockchain-driven sustainability means empowerment of individual actors and a belief that markets will lead to the achievement of optimal states, including environmentally and socially sustainable outcomes.

Tham and Sigala (2020) provide an excellent summary of ways in which blockchain technology can drive sustainability efforts from this neoliberal perspective. They describe its overall ability to "reduce inefficiencies, re-distribute power amongst economic actors and create a more equal playing field between large and small operators" (Tham & Sigala, 2020: 214) and illustrate concrete ways in which blockchain technology can help in achieving sustainable development goals. For example, they argue that blockchain technology empowers tourists, smaller providers, and destinations alike by offering data ownership, choice, and new opportunities to create and translate value. Fostering innovation, supporting fund-raising, and facilitating the establishment of new markets are instrumental steps in which blockchain technology can contribute to sustainable tourism.

Within the overall sustainability context, food waste is one of the most wicked problems in tourism and hospitality (Murphy et al., 2019), and blockchain technology seems to be especially useful in tackling it by helping manage food supply chains. This has been acknowledged by Tham and Sigala (2020) but also by Erol et al. (2022) and Jang, Yoo, and Cho (2023). Food security, transparency, and authenticity are also important topics that have been discussed in connection with blockchain technology, including by Tham and Sigala (2020) and Cozzio et al. (2023). The goal is to foster local food production and consumption, which saves energy costs, provides income for locals, and strengthens local communities. If food has to be acquired through a supply chain, blockchain technology helps with efficiency and traceability. Other areas (e.g., conservation and biodiversity efforts, the prevention of unethical resource extraction, and the protection of cultural heritage and tourism workers) have received very little attention. With ever more imminent consequences of climate change on food supply and for food supply chains, it is expected that the significance of blockchain technology in this context will continue to grow.

One of the big conundrums in relation to blockchain-driven sustainability is the immense energy consumption required for executing the needed computations (Tham & Sigala, 2020). Another one is technology dependence and the often unforeseen consequences of technology use. Who develops the blockchain technology and to whose benefit is a critical issue and one that needs to be urgently discussed. Crandall (2019: 279) argues that "although blockchain is often posed as a revolutionary and disruptive technology, its politics and socio-technical configurations often align with aims to maintain the status quo, and/or aims to concentrate wealth and to make existing powers more efficient", and speaks of "crypto-utopias" and "crypto-colonialism" to describe the rhetoric used in the promotion of blockchain technology.

At the moment, the future of blockchain-driven sustainable tourism looks more like an episode of the Apple TV drama series "Extrapolations", in which tech-savvy billionaires pretend to stand behind sustainability goals in order to push their own, hidden, capitalist agendas. Thus, local communities, responsible tourism businesses, and concerned tourists should watch blockchain developments very closely to make sure they do not empower the wrong kinds of actors. Such vigilance is always recommended in relation to emerging technologies because (as Goethe would put it) the blockchain technology spirits that we've cited can easily ignore our commands. Participatory approaches to blockchain development, as suggested by smart tourism, seem to be important to ensure that achieving sustainability goals through blockchain technology does not just represent a "token" gesture, or worse, could exploit some actors.

Conclusion

The chapter started with quoting Amara's law and with looking at the hype around blockchain technology in general, and specifically in tourism and hospitality.

Literature on blockchain technology in tourism and hospitality has contributed to the hype and the short-term overestimations by being very optimistic and by mostly engaging with conceptualizing its contributions. While there are clearly an increasing number of blockchain-based applications for tourism and hospitality, the industry is far from realizing the full potential of blockchain technology. There are also many issues and shortcomings with the technology (including its enormous energy consumption) that have yet to be resolved and need to be discussed more elaborately and from varying perspectives. However, a long-term impact of blockchain technology on tourism and hospitality is undeniable. The match between tourism and hospitality industry characteristics and needs and blockchain technology capabilities is too perfect to ignore. In addition, major tourism and hospitality initiatives (from smart tourism, to the Metaverse and to sustainable tourism) critically depend on blockchain technology. As these initiatives are moving forward, so will blockchain technology. All these factors together paint a picture of future tourism and hospitality in which blockchain technology will play many major roles.

The specific forms and applications of blockchain technology are still emerging. It will be essential that the various tourism stakeholders realize their ability to shape these developments. In many ways, this chapter should also be seen as a wake-up call for the industry and other stakeholders. Tourism and hospitality players were asleep behind the wheel during a lot of recent technology developments and now have to deal with the consequences. Rather than sitting back and passively observing what might happen in the blockchain space, it is time for tourism and hospitality stakeholders, including academia, to get engaged and actively envision the kind of blockchain technology future they desire. Just because some applications are technologically possible does not mean that they are desirable and beneficial in the long run. Blockchain technology development is a means to developing the kind of tourism and hospitality future we collectively desire, rather than the objective itself.

References

Antoniadis, I., Spinthiropoulos, K., & Kontsas, S. (2020). Blockchain applications in tourism and tourism marketing: A short review. In Kavoura, A., Kefallonitis, E., & Theodoridis, P. (Eds.), *Strategic Innovative Marketing and Tourism: 8th ICSIMAT*, Northern Aegean, Greece, 2019 (pp. 375–384). Cham: Springer.

Balasubramanian, S., Sethi, J. S., Ajayan, S., & Paris, C. M. (2022). An enabling framework for blockchain in tourism. *Information Technology & Tourism, 24*(2), 165–179.

Boes, K., Buhalis, D., & Inversini, A. (2016). Smart tourism destinations: Ecosystems for tourism destination competitiveness. *International Journal of Tourism Cities, 2*(2), 108–124.

Buhalis, D., Leung, D., & Lin, M. (2023). Metaverse as a disruptive technology revolutionising tourism management and marketing. *Tourism Management, 97*, 104724.

Calvaresi, D., Leis, M., Dubovitskaya, A., Schegg, R., & Schumacher, M. (2019). Trust in tourism via blockchain technology: Results from a systematic review. In Pesonen, J., & Neidhardt, J. (Eds.), *Information and Communication Technologies in Tourism 2019:*

Proceedings of the International Conference in Nicosia, Cyprus, January 30–February 1, 2019 (pp. 304–317). Cham: Springer International Publishing.

Cozzio, C., Viglia, G., Lemarie, L., & Cerutti, S. (2023). Toward an integration of blockchain technology in the food supply chain. *Journal of Business Research, 162*, 113909.

Crandall, J. (2019). Blockchains and the "Chains of Empire": Contextualizing blockchain, cryptocurrency, and neoliberalism in Puerto Rico. *Design and Culture, 11*(3), 279–300.

Erol, I., Önder Neuhofer, I., Dogru, T., Oztel, A., Searcy, C., & Yorulmaz, A. C. (2022). Improving sustainability in the tourism industry through blockchain technology: Challenges and opportunities. *Tourism Management, 93*, 104628.

Giesler, M., & Veresiu, E. (2014). Creating the responsible consumer: Moralistic governance regimes and consumer subjectivity. *Journal of Consumer Research, 41*(3), 840–857.

Gretzel, U., Fuchs, M., Baggio, R., Hoepken, W., Law, R., Neidhardt, J., Pesonen, J., Zanker, M., & Xiang, Z. (2020). e-Tourism beyond COVID-19: A call for transformative research. *Information Technology & Tourism, 22*, 187–203.

Gretzel, U., Ham, J., & Koo, C. (2018). Creating the city destination of the future – The case of smart Seoul. In Wang, Y. Shakeela, A., Kwek, A., & Khoo-Lattimore, C. (Eds.), *Managing Asian Destinations* (pp. 199–214). Cham: Springer.

Gretzel, U., & Jamal, T. (2020). Guiding principles for good governance of the smart destination. In Paris, C. M., & Benjamin, S. (Eds.), *Proceedings of the 2020 TTRA International Conference*, June 16–18, 2020, Victoria, BC, Canada. Whitehall, MI: Travel and Tourism Research Association. https://scholarworks.umass.edu/ttra/2020/research_papers/42/.

Gretzel, U., & Koo, C. (2021). Smart tourism cities: A duality of place where technology supports the convergence of touristic and residential experiences. *Asia Pacific Journal of Tourism Research, 26*(4), 352–364.

Gretzel, U., Sigala, M., Xiang, Z., & Koo, C. (2015a). Smart tourism: Foundations and developments. *Electronic Markets, 25*, 179–188.

Gretzel, U., Werthner, H., Koo, C., & Lamsfus, C. (2015b). Conceptual foundations for understanding smart tourism ecosystems. *Computers in Human Behavior, 50*, 558–563.

Hjalager, A. M. (2002). Repairing innovation defectiveness in tourism. *Tourism Management, 23*(5), 465–474.

Irannezhad, E., & Mahadevan, R. (2021). Is blockchain tourism's new hope? *Journal of Hospitality and Tourism Technology, 12*(1), 85–96.

Jang, H. W., Yoo, J. J. E., & Cho, M. (2023). Resistance to blockchain adoption in the foodservice industry: Moderating roles of public pressures and climate change awareness. *International Journal of Contemporary Hospitality Management*. https://doi.org/10.1108/IJCHM-09-2022-1127.

Kwok, A. O., & Koh, S. G. (2019). Is blockchain technology a watershed for tourism development? *Current Issues in Tourism, 22*(20), 2447–2452.

Lacity, M. C., & Treiblmaier, H. (2022). Overview of blockchain technologies. In Lacity, M. C., & Treiblmaier, H. (Eds.), *Blockchains and the Token Economy: Theory and Practice* (pp. 359–365). Cham: Palgrave Macmillan.

Litan, A. (2022). Gartner Hype Cycle for Blockchain and Web3, 2022. https://blogs.gartner.com/avivah-litan/2022/07/22/gartner-hype-cycle-for-blockchain-and-web3-2022/. Accessed April 26, 2023.

Maull, R., Godsiff, P., Mulligan, C., Brown, A., & Kewell, B. (2017). Distributed ledger technology: Applications and implications. *Strategic Change, 26*(5), 481–489.

Murphy, J., Gretzel, U., Pesonen, J., & Elorinne, A. L. (2019). Wicked problem: Reducing food waste by tourist households. *Journal of Gastronomy and Tourism, 3*(4), 247–260.

Nam, K., Dutt, C. S., Chathoth, P., & Khan, M. S. (2021). Blockchain technology for smart city and smart tourism: Latest trends and challenges. *Asia Pacific Journal of Tourism Research, 26*(4), 454–468.

Neuhofer, B., Buhalis, D., & Ladkin, A. (2014). A typology of technology-enhanced tourism experiences. *International Journal of Tourism Research, 16*(4), 340–350.

Önder, I., & Gunter, U. (2022). Blockchain: Is it the future for the tourism and hospitality industry? *Tourism Economics, 28*(2), 291–299.

Önder, I., & Treiblmaier, H. (2018). Blockchain and tourism: Three research propositions. *Annals of Tourism Research, 72*(C), 180–182.

Perren, R., & Kozinets, R. V. (2018). Lateral exchange markets: How social platforms operate in a networked economy. *Journal of Marketing, 82*(1), 20–36.

Raddatz, N., Coyne, J., Menard, P., & Crossler, R. E. (2023). Becoming a blockchain user: Understanding consumers' benefits realisation to use blockchain-based applications. *European Journal of Information Systems, 32*(2), 287–314.

Rashideh, W. (2020). Blockchain technology framework: Current and future perspectives for the tourism industry. *Tourism Management, 80*, 104125.

Revfine (n.d.). Examples of blockchain usage within the hospitality industry. Available at: https://www.revfine.com/blockchain-technology-hospitality-industry/#examples-usage-hospitality-industry. Accessed April 25, 2023.

Ruuska, I., & Teigland, R. (2009). Ensuring project success through collective competence and creative conflict in public–private partnerships–A case study of Bygga Villa, a Swedish triple helix e-government initiative. *International Journal of Project Management, 27*(4), 323–334.

Soares, J. C., Domareski Ruiz, T. C., & Ivars Baidal, J. A. (2022). Smart destinations: A new planning and management approach? *Current Issues in Tourism, 25*(17), 2717–2732.

Tham, A., & Sigala, M. (2020). Road block (chain): Bit (coin) s for tourism sustainable development goals? *Journal of Hospitality and Tourism Technology, 11*(2), 203–222.

Thees, H., Erschbamer, G., & Pechlaner, H. (2020). The application of blockchain in tourism: Use cases in the tourism value system. *European Journal of Tourism Research, 26*, 2602–2602.

Treiblmaier, H. (2020). Blockchain and tourism. In Xiang, Z., Fuchs, M., Gretzel, U., & Höpken, W. (Eds.), *Handbook of e-Tourism*. Cham: Springer. https://doi.org/10.1007/978-3-030-05324-6_28-1.

Treiblmaier, H. (2021). The token economy as a key driver for tourism: Entering the next phase of blockchain research. *Annals of Tourism Research, 91*, 103177.

Um, T., Kim, H., Kim, H., Lee, J., Koo, C., & Chung, N. (2022). Travel Incheon as a metaverse: Smart tourism cities development case in Korea. In Stienmetz, J. L., Ferrer-Rosell, B., & Massimo, D. (Eds.), *Information and Communication Technologies in Tourism 2022: Proceedings of the ENTER 2022 eTourism Conference*, January 11–14, 2022 (pp. 226–231). Cham: Springer International Publishing.

Valeri, M., & Baggio, R. (2021). A critical reflection on the adoption of blockchain in tourism. *Information Technology & Tourism, 23*, 121–132.

Werthner, H., & Klein, S. (1999). *Information Technology and Tourism: A Challenging Relationship*. Wien: Springer-Verlag.

Yang, F. X., & Wang, Y. (2023). Rethinking metaverse tourism: A taxonomy and an agenda for future research. *Journal of Hospitality & Tourism Research*, https://doi.org/10.1177/10963480231163509.

Zach, F. J., Nicolau, J. L., & Sharma, A. (2020). Disruptive innovation, innovation adoption and incumbent market value: The case of Airbnb. *Annals of Tourism Research, 80*, 102818.

INDEX

Note: **Bold** page numbers refer to tables and *italic* page numbers refer to figures.

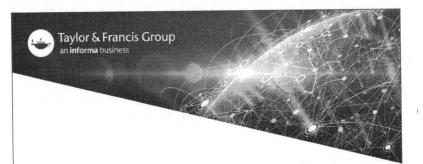

Printed in the United States
by Baker & Taylor Publisher Services